How to start production motorcycle racing

By Ray Knight

First impression March 1973.
(Parts of this book first appeared in "Racing and Tuning
Production Motorcycles")

ISBN 0 85113 065 8

Published by
Speedsport Motobooks
(Interauto Book Company Limited)
Bercourt House, York Road, Brentford,
Middlesex, TW8 OQP, England.

Printed in Great Britain by
HGA Printing Company Ltd.,
Brentford, Middlesex.

Contents

Introduction:

This is a revised and updated edition of the book 'Racing and Tuning Production Motorcycles'. Since the writing of that book in 1969 new machines have come to prominence and the regulations governing this branch of the sport have changed a little. There are new chapters on Formula 750 class racing and the racing schools. The chapters have been revised and the regulations and machine specifications have a chapter to themselves. Production racing continues to flourish, to those tempted to try their hand — why not?

Chapter 1
Why production racing?

The fact that you are reading this book suggests that you are an enthusiastic motorcyclist with high speed aspirations, or at least an interest in things racing and want to know more about it. You probably have a bike of your own, will have been to a race meeting and are wondering, however vaguely, just how do you start racing. Could you? If this first paragraph fits then the answer is yes and it is spelt out in detail in the following pages.

Why production racing anyway? If for no other reason than that production racing offers the cheapest way of making your deput on the tarmac, and the easiest too. Naturally though, most of the information given applies equally well to open class and Formula 750 racing, with the exception of machine details.

But before committing yourself to the idea of having a go with a production bike you might like to know something of the scope for the class and of its background and development.

Production racing may now fairly be called a branch of motorcycle racing sport in Its own right. It is possible to spend almost every weekend racing a roadster on some circuit or other, there are Natlonal events in increasing number, Club Championships to be won, British International status events, the TT and even a Continental marathon series in which to compete, of which our own Motor Cycle Thruxton 500 Mile Grand Prix forms part.

The present popularity of production racing can trace its origins in the first Thruxton Nine Hour Race, held for the first time in 1955. Staged, as it is now, by the Southampton and District Motorcycle Club, it has progressed from a chance for the clubmen of the day to give sporting roadsters an outing to a works supported Grand Prix with sales and prestige in the balance.

The event grew and it was not long before works prepared machinery appeared. In 1957 Bob McIntire rode a Royal Enfield and in 1958 an up and very much coming lad named Hailwood rode a 650 Triumph as one of the stepping stones to stardom. In 1959 a BMW scored a win and the race was firmly established in the calendar and supported by the trade. Also in 1959 the state of Grand Prix racing was in such decline that a class had to be introduced in the Isle of Man

Tourist Trophy Races for Formula One machines. These were the over the counter racers produced by Norton, Matchless and A.J.S. This was the official recognition that British racing machinery was so outclassed by the Italian multi-cylinder machines that it stood no chance of offering any sort of challenge on even terms, only by default could it win, when the all-conquering MV Augusta suffered a rare bout of mechanical trouble. Though this race was not to be repeated, another that was, was the British Motorcycle Racing Club's Production race, included in their Trophy Day races at Silverstone. This immediately proved popular and now every 'Bemsee' meeting has a well supported race for roadsters and soon other clubs were following suit as clubmen found in their ride-to-work machines a means of competing without having to buy a special racing machine, just to see if they could really do any good on the track.

A premature step in the development of the class came in 1961 when Bemsee instituted their ill-fated 1,000 Kilometre race on the Grand Prix circuit at Silverstone. Competitor and trade support were forthcoming but spectator interest was not, and on the financial success this depended. 1962 was little better but again bad weather and few supporters and the event shifted to Oulton Park for 1963 in a bid to save it. But it seems that the public were not yet ready to welcome more than one marathon into the calendar.

But while the 500 Miler went from strength to strength the current British racing scene continued to stagnate, and then the Honda invasion of the world's racing circuits began to further emphasise the shortcomings of the available racing machinery that could be bought. With the disappearance of the Manx Norton, AJS 7R and Matchless G50 from the market, the British demise from the racing scene was complete, but the way began to open for something to take its place.

Another landmark in the development of production racing came in 1965 when both Triumph and Velocette introduced models intended for the job. They were fitted with all the necessary parts to suit them to the task and there were many additions to the specification of the standard model. Both were named after the Thruxton circuit, respectively Thruxton Velocette Venom and Thruxton Bonneville. This was the first real sign of the manufacturers coming out in the open and supporting production racing, or even acknowledging officially that it existed. Velocettes went on to make a real success of the model but Triumphs seem to have quietly dropped the name Thruxton from the catalogue thereafter.

However, trade entered but obvious works machines appeared in the following seasons and it was an open secret that the various 'works' were taking more than a passing interest.

6

When in 1967 a production race was included in the TT programme the class had really arrived. Up until then the stigma of 'playing at racers' had been dying hard. The more serious racers had long regarded production racing in this light and the tag of the café racer, which had never been deserved, was a hard one to live down. Now there are official works entries from Norton with a strong supporting field backed by the trade. The lap record stands at over 101 mph and the entry are all experienced men who are certainly not playing at racers.

With long years of seeing the same machine race around the circuits the viewing public is ready to welcome variety in the race programmes. Racers starved of British machinery for many years and now faced with the prospects of paying £900 plus for Seeley or Manx machines, or go foreign, are seeing in production bikes the possibility of cheaper racing. It would seem that the rise in support for the class grew as the GP racing scene declined. As real racing engines ceased to be available production engines were grafted in to racing cycles and it came to be accepted that a basically touring unit could give sufficient performance to compete on even terms with famous names like Norton and Matchless. But that is really Formula 750 racing, of which has a chapter of its own.

Manufacturers who had refused to be drawn into racing saw in the increasing acceptance of production racing the means of obtaining prestige using basically stock machines and their development behind the scenes, and that of the ever enthusiastic band of dealer entrants in the trade, led to the production of machines which steered and stopped in a very much superior fashion to those of only a few years ago.

Though there are now some long awaited signs that the Grand Prix racing scene is undergoing one of its periodic hints of revival, production racing has reaped the fruits of its earlier decline to become part of the racing scene at an International level and anyone contemplating taking it up can now be assured that there are more than sufficient events to keep a machine for the job well employed, but more to the point, it now offers a real means of achieving progress at the top of the racing tree.

Fig. 1 — A very standard looking 250 Yamaha. Owned and ridden by Jim Evans it was good enough to put up a fine performance at the 1972 Motorcycle 500 Mile Race at Thruxton, where only a reversal of the official lap scoring after the race robbed him of the class win.

Chapter 2
Getting onto the grid

So you have decided to have a go at racing. How do you join in the fun, what does one have to do to get onto the grid? Well before rushing on to talk about the bikes, tuning and riding I'm afraid that one has to complete various formalities before you get around to facing the Union Jack.

Right from the start you have to join a club because the rules of the game compel you to start at the least competitive level, appropriately enough. So you have to find a club that actually oragnises race meetings at the place where you wish to compete, and make sure that they do have a production class, most do but not all.

To enter a race, first fill in an entry form - elementary my dear Watson. But where do you get those from? The Secretary of the Meeting. And this hard working volunteer clubman spends a lot of his time mailing out sets of regulations to all racing club members - and they don't all race, a lot of people have to put in their spare time to get you that place on the grid. Perhaps their satisfaction comes from helping to organise race meetings.

So you joined the right club and the Secretary has placed you on the mailing list for those regulations (regs). Now when you get them, so will the rest of the club members and the chances are that there are more bodies with bikes ready to race in the class that you have chosen, than there are available places on the grid. So the chances are that somebody is going to be unlucky. In club racing the entries are accepted by the Secretary as they are received, first come first served.

Everything you can do to make sure that your entry gets there early helps to ensure that you will be there on the day. You pay for your entry with postal orders or cheques, usually made out to the organising club, or occasionally to the organising secretary. Now 'by return' must be the rule to get in first, and if for instance you get home from wherever and the regs are on the mat it may well be that you can find a post box somewhere in the district that has that late collection, around 7.30, probably the branch PO. So if you grab the forms, fill them in and get them back in the post that night (First Class) the secretary will have them the next morning. Well the chances are that you cannot get the right postal orders at the drop of a hat and so I have found it's well worthwhile to have a cheque book, be it only the smallest 'working account', so you can complete the entry as soon as possible.

Having given yourself the best possible chance of getting accepted you may still not get in straightaway. You could have your entry returned 'oversubscribed', no explanation required, have it 'held in abeyance' - which means the secretary is holding it in case he can fit it in at the last moment due to withdrawal by another, already accepted competitor, in which case you are at liberty to apply somewhere else for a race on that day, but you must write and say so. Lastly you can be accepted as a 'reserve entry'. This means that you will at least get as far as practising on the day to qualify for the race, but it is still possible that you might not get a ride. Reserves are accepted, and the number varies from club to club, to replace those competitors who may have machine trouble in practice and cannot turn out for the race, or perhaps the van broke-down on the way to the circuit - or they may even still be in bed. However, the rules permit just so many competitors on the track at one time so, should everybody turn-up then the reserves will not get a ride. But I have usually found that I have got in so if you do get reserve do not despair.

If you do not race then you will of course have your money refunded. But only the entry fee, not the insurance portion. This is because having already practised you have been 'on risk'. Had you crashed in practice you would have received the benefits you insured for and you can hardly expect to get back money that you have spent.

Incidently, the number of competitors on a track is decided by the application of a formula that is worked out on the width and length of a circuit to prevent overcrowding. At the Brands Hatch 1.25 mile circuit, 28 starters are permitted on the grid, while in the Isle of Man there can be 100 - but that circuit is the best part of 40 miles long. This rule is relaxed somewhat for production machine marathon events like the 500 mile race. A normal race at the Thruxton circuit could have 40 starters, but this is increased to 60, as with racing going on for about six hours, mechanical failures soon take their toll and reduce the numbers.

But back to the paperwork. Everybody who gets an entry accepted has to be sent paddock passes and final instructions which will, among other things, advise you of your racing numbers. So there are lots of tickets and forms to be stuffed into hundreds of envelopes and posted - quite a job.

In developing the desire to have a go at racing you may have been induced to start by visiting a track to spectate, by knowing of somebody else who races and reckoning you can do as well, or by just reading about racing in the several papers and magazines devoted to the sport. Which ever way, you probably have the wish to race at a certain track, if only because it's the nearest one. How to do it? First find out which clubs organise events at that particular track. If there is nobody to hand that can enlighten you, race reports in the press mention the name of the organising club, from there you need the name of the club Secretary to whom you should write for details of membership and races. This is the first unpaid, voluntary club official that you will come into contact with and if you do not get a reply 'by return', it's worth remembering that he probably spends all his spare time answering and writing letters to members, and potential members - so send him a stamped, addressed envelope. But you might not have his address - what then? And you might wish to enter in a National status event rather than a club race.

You will need now to contact the organising body of motorcycle road racing in this country, The Auto Cycle Union. Write to the Secretary, 31 Belgrave Square, London, WC2, requesting the name and address you require, you might also take the opportunity to request the forms required to obtain a National Competition Licence. Now it is not possible to enter a National status event without a competition licence, and since one has to qualify for one of these you cannot make an entry among what is potentially a field of star riders until you have acquired certain experience on the track. You might otherwise well be in danger by virtue of inexperience, to yourself and others. To obtain the required experience you must have raced in, and completed, three club races and have had your National Licence application form signed by the organising official, the Clerk of the Course, to certify that this is so. So back to square one and join the necessary club.

Apart from needing to be an amateur mechanic, racing rider, driver and tuner, you will develop some small aptitude for clerical work and organisation too, at least if you do much more than a little racing. If you only belong to one or two clubs, your regulations may well arrive automatically, as the secretary will send them out to all racing members - so no problem. However let's assume that you are looking forward to your first full season and the racing calendar has just been published in the press. You'll decide how many races you want to go in for and where, and make yourself a list of the dates, circuits and club secretaries and their addresses, or those of the organisers if the event is higher status than 'closed to club'. This, not too surprisingly, means that only club members can compete.

The next one up the list, so to speak, is a Regional Restricted event, run by a club but open to members of all clubs within a certain area. 'Closed to Centre' are similar but this means that members of clubs within Auto Cycle Union Centres designated as SE, SW, etc., are eligible.

Next comes a National event which is open to all holders of a National Competition Licence, where you may well get all the big names competing. An International means that foreign riders can compete and also that holders of that class of licence will have qualified for it by certain successes in National events.

There is some competition to get an entry for many events above Club status and only so many entry forms are likely to be sent out by the Secretary. Consequently unless you make your request for the regulations in good time, you will miss out. Especially if you happen to be a newcomer and the Secretary has never heard of you. He has the job of getting the best possible entry in order to attract spectators and ensure good racing. If 10 Mike Hailwoods want to ride you must sympathise with the man if he accepts those entries first and you are 11th on the list. So to give yourself the best chance of getting the regs., send him a stamped addressed envelope, clearly marked on the back with your name, the date of the meeting and the circuit - he may have several meetings to run - and the machine you want to enter and be sure that he has it about 11 weeks before the date of the meeting.

Now you will get an idea why you need the list. Firstly you will need to check on your sending of the request for regulations and the dates to post them off, when you have actually entered and if you get accepted. Otherwise the permutations for getting everything mixed up are endless. You can enter for two meetings on the same day but be warned, you can lose your competition licence if you do that. Or you can think you've entered, or forget to send the forms in because some meetings have an 'opening date'. Now that means that no entries should be sent in before a certain date, this is to avoid favouring those with a better postal service, so you carefully put them on one side and wait for the day, other regs turn up meanwhile and presto! You forget. The other date is a 'closing date'. This is just the date after which no more entries will be accepted anyway, because the organiser has got to be able to list all the competitors and get the information off to the printer who wants time to print the programmes.

Some clubs will actually accept entries on the day of the race; then you will find that the closing date for regs is the same as that of the meeting. It is only done by a few of the clubs and it makes hard work for them with bodies busy taking money and filling in forms on the day. And if you do want an entry on the day the grid may well be full anyway, so don't rely on it.

Another item of paperwork you will run up against is a request for 'change of machine'. Should you perchance change your bike between the time of entering and the day of the race you must get permission from the Clerk of the Course for this to be allowed. Mike Hailwood was once pulled out of a race when he was out in front for not registering a change of machine. Just take a slip of paper address it to the C of C and simply request the substitution of bike 'A' for bike 'B'.

One more piece of paper that I hope you don't have to employ is the 'protest'. There could be a multitude of reasons for feeling that you were the victim of some injustice. It might be anything from what you felt to be another competitor's unfair driving to a decision by a race official that you thought was unjust. It might be that somebody was using 'pirate' components. Either way, the official way to raise the matter is to write out a formal protest, which must be accompanied by the one pound required for so doing, and your case will be considered by the Auto Cycle Union officials. The pound is merely to prevent frivolous protests and will be returned as long as it was not considered to be so.

But you are still no nearer getting on to the grid and since that is the name of this chapter we'll skip some ground and assume that you have an entry. The great day has arrived, you are in the paddock and the first chore is to get the machine passed by the scrutineer, also your leathers, boots and helmet. So it's into the queue and be sure that it's in good time because practice usually follows quickly after this and you have to get into your leathers, warm-up the motor and be in the collecting area ready to go at the appointed time.

Scrutineers are a sorely abused body of officials who sometimes have the unenviable job of preventing you from racing for the sake of your own safety. Should they find that the machine possesses a feature that would be a source of hazard to you, and therefore the others who might be involved in an incident, you may have the bike rejected. More likely they will find some small defect that requires a quick remedy at the time and will let you through on the understanding that you rectify it before practice. When the bike and clothing are okayed you will be required to 'sign on', as well as giving another signature to declare that you are 100% fit to participate, to the best of your knowledge. Some clubs then issue you with a ticket that will allow you to practice and you will not get out onto the circuit without it. This is done to prevent indiscriminate use of the circuit, as there is only limited time available before racing starts - and you want your share of time on the track.

As you go to the collecting area you'll meet another golden hearted volunteer who makes the day's racing possible, the Paddock Marshal. And here it's very well worthwhile considering trying a few marshalling duties to give you an insight into the racing game. A few meetings by the trackside could teach you more than all the reading might. The Paddock Marshal may well turn you away, that is if you are attempting to join the wrong crowd going out for practice.

Fig. 2 – The two works Norton production racing Commandos in the paddock at Silverstone. Note the twin exhausts on the right hand side of the machines, a style adopted by the works in '72: 'lines of exhaust systems may be varied as long as the diameter of the pipe is not changed or silencer interfered with.

They might be sending out the 125cc racing machines for instance, and there is a specified time for the production bikes to go out, so just make sure you are in the right lot. But just to make life difficult some clubs require production bikes to practice with their respective capacity classes.

So why should it matter? Well it is a requirement that you must practice before being allowed to race. This is to give you a chance to learn the circuit. You could not expect to ride on the limit if you didn't know what the next corner was like, rushing into it off line too fast could be the start of a nasty accident, involving others as well as yourself.

So how do 'they' know that you have practised? Well all the classes of racing machines have different colour number plates to indicate their capacity and when you do go out then the timekeepers will check off your number as you go by. Imagine the confusion if there were four bikes in a line out there with the same numbers but different colours. Bikes come by the timekeeper's box in bunches at high speed and the numbers are difficult enough to catch without duplication and having to spot colours too. Since you could be missed in the confusion you could appear on the notice board as a non-starter, and that could cost you your race so make sure you do join the right class.

So whats with all this paperwork, scrutineers, marshal's telling you what to do and all the rules and regulations. After all you only want to race and without giving matters much thought easily take offence at people who are organising you so its not a bad idea to know whats behind all the fuss before you can get onto the grid. When you know why a thing should be, then its easier to comply willingly.

Many months before the meeting, even a year or so, the Secretary will have been involved in obtaining circuit bookings from track owners for the season to come, so you can see that the administrative work has been going on for months before. Regulations will have been drafted and a programme worked out for the day's racing. Not just by the Secretary of course, a committee of six or seven are required to cope with all the work that goes into organising a season's racing. Just consider the work behind getting a grid full of competitors to the line. First there may be several hundred sets of regulations to be sent out, and they have all to be printed. That's something that will probably be done by the club volunteers as well, rolling all the forms off on a hand duplicator. Then there are all the envelopes to be filled, and possibly addressed by hand. That is unless the club has a system of getting members to send in stamped addressed envelopes or addressed sticky labels. In either event it's an evening's chore for at least a couple of bodies. When all the completed sets of forms come pouring back through somebody's letterbox there commences the job of sorting them out into all the other classes - as well as the production races, returning those forms incorrectly filled in and allocating riding numbers.

While all the paperwork is being processed, the Chief Marshal is working on the unenviable task of ensuring that there are enough enthusiasts there on the day to stand by at all the danger points and risk life and limb for the pleasure of picking you up if you fall off. They might well have to stand out in the rain and cold all day to do it too. If there are not enough volunteers available to do the job there just won't be any racing, because one of the reasons why there has to be an ACU Steward to supervise the meeting is to ensure that all safety precautions are observed, and adequate marshals are one of the first considerations.

So now maybe you will appreciate that a lot of work by lots of unpaid enthusiasts goes into getting you onto the grid. The multitude of marshals and other officials are all there to see that the racing is as safe as it can be made for you - and even in spite of you in a few cases. You will come across the badly prepared machine and impatient rider. If the machine has a fault that slips through scrutineering making it potentially dangerous then it will be because people are fallible. If the impatient rider pushes his luck then you hope that there is a well ordered sequence of events that will clear him and his bike from your path. It all needs organisation.

Chapter 3

What does it cost?

So now you know how to go about getting that place on the grid. But whats it going to cost? Can you really afford to go racing?

Almost everything costs money. Sports and pleasures inevitably seem to come at the top of the list when it comes to paying the bills. Motorcycle racing is far from an exception and must, unfortunately, rank as one of the more expensive although to a considerable degree it is dependent on just how ambitious you are. If you seek the honour of being first past the flag then you obviously need the fastest machinery available because the winner is on something quick, and it's him you have to beat. While you could easily spend £1,300 plus on the latest thing in racing machines from Japan, and hundreds of £££s on a transporter, production racing does offer by comparison an inexpensive alternative.

At the lesser end of the scale, competitively and financially, you can use the bike you use on the road and, with modifications carried out by yourself and with no more tools than you would reasonably expect any enthusiast to have, get on the track and have a try to find out if racing is what you expect it to be. This is probably the greatest thing that the production class has to offer. Trying your hand at racing before you buy a special machine for the job. Buy a racer and you may find that it is not what you expected and lose a great deal of money in the process. Of course, if you do buy an 'open' racer then you must be able to transport it to the meeting.

Your roadster in production racing trim can be ridden to the meeting, because after all, nothing that you do to it should make it unsuitable for road use, indeed almost that very phrase is in the regulations drawn up by the ACU governing production racing. There are, in fact, still a few lads about who ride their bikes to the meetings, fit racing number plates, tape up lamp glasses, remove stands - and race - and not unsuccessfully either. So you see you have the chance of really getting into the game before costs get prohibitive.

Costs of new machines, if you are lucky enough to have the cash available, are tackled in the chapter entitled 'What to race?' Secondhand ones, are of course, available and may be found in dealers' showrooms at the end of a season or advertised in the columns of the relevant magazines and papers. There is much

Fig. 3 — This Triumph Trident lapped Silverstone at over 100 mph in the hands of Triumph works tester Percy Tait. It finished second in the production race behind a similar model ridden by Ray Pickrell. The Fontana front brake is a homologated optional extra as specified by the factory.

to be said for buying a secondhand machine because all the work needed to put it into competition trim should have been carried out. If you buy a brand new one it has still to be prepared for the track and, if you choose to go the whole hog and order one to be prepared to competition standards that could cost you many more pounds. And of course it is possible to get all the preparation done for you. There are always people in the trade who will carry out any sort of work - for a price. The best people to go to, for work or advice, are those dealers who are enthusiastic enough about the sport to enter and race their own machine or give a measure of support to lads already racing.

Now when your enthusiasm for the sport reaches a certain point you will probably want to confine the riding of your production racer to the track, which means transporting it. A visit to any paddock will show you how this job is tackled. Fifteen hundredweight commercial vans seem to be the most popular. These will take up to three big models, tools, spares and often wives and families plus camping gear for the weekend's racing. If you know enough about four wheeled vehicles, buying one for £100 upwards and sharing it with a mate can make the proposition quite reasonable in terms of economics.

Something like a Ford, Bedford or Austin van can give up to 25mpg and enough performance to make long distances feasible - the circuits you want to race at always seem to be many miles away. A couple of hundred miles in a day is quite a modest mileage, some competitors will do 400 or 500 to attend a particular event in a weekend. Of course, fuel and oil are not the only things. Anyway, after fuel for the transporter there's fuel for the racer, and you still have to eat. Meals bought on the road are not too bad but restaurants in paddocks, if there are any, are not cheap, and meals for two or three for the day can cost quite a few bob. Soup in a thermos and sandwiches are a reasonable alternative but if you do have a van then it's easy to get a calor or paraffin stove going and have a fry-up, as you will find most competitors doing during a racing day.

Vans are a blessing, particularly when the weather is bad. On a wet day each one becomes a clubhouse. If you have trouble in practice you can even get a bike inside and work on it in the dry, which is something you can't do in a car.

However, be that as it may, you might well have a car to start off with and to buy a van as well is hardly cheap racing. You might even have a friend who will lend the services of a car for the day. In any case you'll need a trailer to carry the bike on.

Trailers can cost you anything up to £50 for one to carry two or three bikes, if you must have a new one professionally built, but that's the expensive way of doing things. Far better to find yourself a secondhand one and once again these can be found in the columns of the papers, or build your own from parts bought through the Exchange & Mart. A cautionary word though, if you are towing, be sure your insurance covers you, it doesn't always.

We have dealt with most of the ways of getting the racer to the circuit, including riding it. There is one more way though, a float - or to be more precise, a combination with box sidecar to carry the bomb in. In fact I used this method myself for a while, though my 'chair outfit' was used to pull a tiny trailer with 8in wheels that was nevertheless, man enough to take the 700cc Royal Enfield that I was racing at the time. The old Triumph Thunderbird doing the pulling coped very well, but it was well geared down for doing the job.

Well, all the foregoing is an aspect that is seldom covered in books on the subject but the mere expense of just getting yourself and bike t / the circuit can be considerable, and then you have to eat. In fact they are some of the often forgotten costs of racing. One aspect of finance that you won't forget however is entry fees. club memberships, licence and insurance costs. At one end of the scale it could cost you £8 to enter a production TT race and £5 for a marathon event like the 500 Mile Race, but they will certainly be out for a while, at least until you have qualified for the necessary licence.

You will obviously be more interested in club races to start with. Now the British Motorcycle Racing club (referred to as Bemsee) is the only one with a full-time professional staff. They have to be paid like you and I so to enter a Bemsee race will probably cost you more than to enter a race with any other club. A Bemsee race will cost you about £2 per race, but it does not end there, you have also to pay for the obligatory insurance coverage. Yes you have to be insured for every race and that can cost you £1.5p, making £3.5p for just one race - say seven laps at the Snetterton circuit or 10 at Brands Hatch club circuit.

Insurance makes the racing game sound dangerous. Motorcycle racing is dangerous - of course, but dangerous compared with what? It's dangerous enough to cross a busy main road and assuming that you already ride on the open roads, racing can actually be less dangerous than this in many cases.

Certainly the consequences of making an error of judgement while racing can be far less disastrous, there is always somebody close at hand to pick you up - or even patch you up, on the road anything can happen. But a Bemsee event is the most expensive of club events, though since they dish out the most awards you can't have it all ways. Other clubs only require a £1 or so for an entry fee and so on up, but then they don't have salaries to pay and offices to run.

Preventive Maintenance

Now you might not think that this item came under costs, but it certainly does. Riding on the road you replace a component when it shows signs of wear, on the track such a policy could easily cost you very much more than that of replacing worn parts. After having used a machine for a busy season's racing - perhaps 30-40 events, I am in the habit of replacing certain major components like connecting rod for instance to prevent metal fatigue taking its toll, resulting probably in broken crankcases as well. When they were designed they were stressed to cope with all the demands of a normal machine's lifetime on road usage, but racing imposes far greater stresses.

This is not to say that one does not do the same thing on a racing machine. Valves for instance, usually have a recommended certain life before replacement, and another item which, particularly on a production bike should be watched closely, is the primary chain. On a Bonneville for instance, I'd change the primary chain at least once during a season. For the rear chain, while disasters due to breakages are less liable, the spring link should be checked frequently as it is the weakest link of all. Indeed in long races this is dispensed with, a link is rivetted in place to make the chain endless and remove one possible cause of failure.

So preventative maintenance is something that is to be considered as a racing expense, one more item for the balance sheet, as also are tyres. These are covered in the chapter on preparation, but from the costs angle the high performance road tyres like the Dunlop/TT100 or Avon Grand Prix offer the longest life obtainable while providing enough adhesion for serious racing. Some bikes even fit them on the front wheel though they are intended for the rear. For instance, they are popular on the front of the Norton Commando, the 3.60 by 19 size being used. Some racers though prefer a racing cover on the front and these wear out very much quicker, in fact an afternoon spent practising at some of the more abrasively surfaced tracks like Brands Hatch, and you are nearly ready for a replacement.

Sponsorship

It would be a lucky man - there are just a few girls racing - indeed who discovered a sponsor when he started racing, but you'll certainly hear about them. You'll probably have seen so-and-so shown in the programme as entered by Joe Bloggs motors. The lucky rider will have most of his cost problems solved for him because in all probability even if he is not riding somebody else's bike then Joe Bloggs motors are probably paying his entry fees and helping out with maintenance and spares.

Finding a sponsor is every club racer's dream, and they are few and far between. At least one way in is to patronise one's particular dealer for your spares, if you are racing you'll spend plenty of time in his shop and he'll soon get to know you. If you do achieve any success on the track you might even persuade him to offer a measure of support. But if he is at all enthusiastic you won't be the only one in the queue.

Yes you actually have to pay to race and in some instances pay to entertain spectators who in any case are paying to come in and see you do your bit on the track, and it sounds a bit off I know. But there are exceptions and though you'll have to cover a lot of ground and win many races before being one of the exceptions, it's nice to know about start money. When you have achieved something like stardom, your name will be a big enough attraction for the organisers to actually pay you to appear on the starting grid so that they can use your name in pre-race advertising to draw in the crowds. I know, for instance, that a regular fee for Mike Hailwood was once £500, but then he would draw in enough spectators to more than repay that sum.

Chapter 4

Personal equipment

If you have spectated at many meetings, you will, almost inevitably, have seen some unfortunate competitor come unstuck and slide along the tarmac, and with a little luck pick himself up and be sufficiently unscathed to worry first about the condition of the bike, and then himself. This fortunate state of affairs is almost certainly due to the protective clothing worn, therefore its condition and fit is vital to your wellbeing, as vital as the fitness of your machine for its job. Therefore, when the bike is checked over by the scrutineer so will your clothing be checked, checked to see that it will be able to do the job that you hope it will not have to do.

Probably the most important item is your helmet and if you have been using your present one on the road for some time it's a good idea to start off with a new one. Economy here is false - even fatal. A good one can cost anything up to £30 for the dearest thing that money can buy in 'space helmets' from America.

The accepted standard for helmet testing in the States is the Snell Foundation. The standards laid down by this body are said to be so rigorous that the majority of British helmets are not accepted by the Americans as safe for racing. For instance they do not accept our 'pudding basin' style at all, insisting that the additional protection afforded by the space type to the temples and ears is a must. Indeed the old style of helmet is now banned from the tracks in this country too.

The approval of the American Snell foundation is now accepted in this country by the ACU but even so such a helmet must still bear the ACU seal of approval. This approval takes several forms, from perforations in the helmet's harness to a transfer on the shell, or even a tab sewn in to the harness somewhere, that itself bears the mark of certification, and it is this that the scrutineer will be looking for first when he examines it, as well as for signs of deterioration.

Whichever sort you have, or intend getting, it is the sign of approval that it will have to bear before it will be accepted for racing. You can buy a model that is of itself approved but has not individually been submitted to the ACU for approval and does not have the mark on it. So when you buy a new one you have to specify that it bears the approval.

You may wonder whether your present model is still up to racing if you have had it for some time. 'The glass fibre shell may last anything up to five years', is the quote from one manufacturer, provided that it is properly cared for'. This proviso was made with the reservation the harness might need renewing every couple of years to make sure that it is in the peak of condition. It is easily affected by an excess of hair dressing for instance. Anyway, this method is very much cheaper than buying a new model.

Goggles

From helmets to goggles, and if worn glasses. They must both be 'made from unsplinterable material'. Goggles are fairly obvious. The lens will probably be made like a car windscreen, using toughened and laminated glass, or even one of the plastic materials. Either way, if you buy a space-type helmet make sure that they will fit comfortably inside it, interference here is common and you may need a model that is not so wide.

As a regular wearer, spectacles can pose problems. It is possible to get goggles made up with prescription lenses, you'll find adverts in the papers for those, or your optician can supply special specs. with the lens made of safety glass or one of the latest 'unbreakable' plastics. If you do get special ones made up be sure to get a certificate with them to certify that the lens are indeed unbreakable because you may one day be asked by a race official for proof that this is so, as per regulations. An alternative is contact lenses. These will dispose of the misting up problem, doubly so with glasses. Of the two types, micro-corneal and the 'small saucer' variety that cover the whole eyeball, probably the later are the more suitable, as it's so easy to lose the micro type if your goggles do mist up and you have to pull them down, the wind could then blow this type off, or they could easily become dislodged if you have a spill.

The big ones actually offer a certain amount of mechanical protection to the eyeball and with them it is quite possible to dispense with goggles completely in the rain if you have a fairing. However, they are difficult to fit and it takes a time for the eye to become accustomed to wearing them, you might never acquire sufficient tolerance from them for the job. Whatever you wear, when it looks like rain give goggles and spec's a good demisting treatment with one of the several solutions on the market for the job.

I have not mentioned visors yet and these really do offer a solution to the vision problem in wet weather though these too should be demisted. The same applies to the visor fitted to the 'full frontal' type of helmet.

Leathers

Leathers can cost you anything up to £40, or even more for a de luxe set with all the latest colour trimmings. Cheaper sets come from about £30 and it is possible to get a 10 per cent discount with some of the outfitters if you belong to certain racing clubs. If you are buying a new set then it is definitely worth getting them made to measure, comfort can be everything in a long race - and you will no doubt want to do the marathon events sometime. You could quite well fall in the 'impecunious enthusiast' bracket, and which of us does not when starting to race? The alternative to a new made to measure set is of course a secondhand set. These can often be found by studying the columns of the motor cycling press, which often have a column for clothing. You could strike lucky and find a set for as little as £10-£15, but do make sure that they fit properly. Try them on - you only wear underwear underneath them, and make sure that you can assume the racing crouch position in them. The time to find a set is at the end of a season when people are retiring and selling up.

It's not required that leathers must in fact be made of leather. As yet, there is no better substitute, but it is possible to find PVC sets. Make sure that they bear the ACU stamp of approval though, rather in a similar manner to helmets.

These suits are not very popular, though I guess that in the rain they could have distinct advantages.

Gloves

Gloves are a most important item in the protective armoury. If you do hit the deck the chances are that you will do some of the sliding on your hands and I don't think that I need to dwell on the possibilities if these are wafer thin, as some of them are. Your normal riding gauntlets are OK for a try, even mitts, in fact on a cold and wet Autumn day you could well be grateful of the extra warmth.

Boots

Boots are largely a matter of individual preference. Many riders wear racing boots on the road anyway. One thing you cannot do on the track though is to wear boots with studs or steel toe caps, or tips on the heels. Imagine the effects that sparks from these would produce upon petrol on the track spilt by a crash !

25

Fig. 4 — Honda CB 750s are a comparitive rarity around the circuits but they go well enough with only slight modifications to be competitive. The self-starter is a distinct advantage. This one is ridden by Hugh Evans and entered by Ongar M/Cs of Essex, it's performing at Silverstone's wide open spaces in the International John Player meeting.

With the angles of lean that modern tyres permit, it's not unusual to see riders' boots bevelled right off at the sides to the extent of leaving toes poking through. Then the adhesive tape that you see wound around some of the boots will be explained. In case you join that brigade it's well to warn you that while you may get away with it most times, you could also be rejected if a scrutineer catches you at it. Even when you get on the grid it's been known for competitors to be turned away with this one. One thing, don't get boots that are so short that they leave a gap between them and your leathers.

Face masks

A last item under the heading of clothing is face masks. These can be very useful if you are inclined to rub your chin along the tarmac, and I suppose it could happen to any of us. Similarly if it happens to be sheeting with rain, and the raindrops feel like tin tacks at speed, you'll be very glad that you have a mask. Masks come in two varieties of fitting, and two more of coverage. One sort is fixed by fitting press studs to the harness of the helmet, while the other has elastic straps that pass around your head. Of the two sorts of coverage, the first comes just up to your lips while the other covers everything up to your goggles. Of course there is the - still favoured by some - handkerchief knotted round your neck. At least it costs nothing but it can't give the protection of leather.

Oversuits

Fully kitted out now you may be, but when race day dawns so often the heavens open up, and they don't stop the racing either. You will see some of the other riders wearing one-piece oversuits of 'barbour-type' material. Then you will think that they are worth their weight in gold because there is little worse than spending the day in, or struggling in and out of, wet leathers. They are not very waterproof and take at least a week to dry out properly, and this must be done slowly or you will ruin them.

Well such an oversuit costs somewhere about £10-£12 depending on the make you choose. Of course most two-piece suits could serve but it's surprising how much difference it makes to the top speed being properly streamlined and being tucked away, rather than sitting partially upright because you can't really get down to it with the bulk of the clothing that you have on. After all the idea is to obtain the last mph possible and a race does not last more than a few minutes, so some do not bother and put up with getting wet. Here it's worth noting that leathers are best kept regularly treated with one of the special oils available for the job which does make them a little more waterproof.

The last item of personal equipment is a personal identification disc. If the worst comes to the worst and you are carted off in an ambulance in a hurry then either the police or the hospital will want your personal details and you may be in no fit state to tell them. If there are two or three of you they might know who was taken away but not who is who. So you will want one with your name and address and date of birth on it and it is also recommended that you include your blood group as well. It could save your neck if minutes are vital. In fact in some events you will have to be able to quote it in order to be able to race anyway so you might as well get it done in the first place and be prepared for those International races later on.

These are usually worn around the neck on a chain but also may be worn on the wrist, but I'm not in favour of that as you can lose them if you slide down the track. Incidently if your Doctor wants to charge you the earth to test your blood to find out what type it is you can always be a blood donor for once then they will tell you your group, and costs you nothing.

Chapter 5
Preparing the bike

This is not intended to be a magical treatise on how to obtain lots more mph from your standard roadster. There are better books than I could possibly write on motor tuning already on the market. Rather is it intended to be the basics of preparation that should be carried out before taking your machine to the track, to ensure that your efforts do not result in unforeseen disaster to machine or person.

As good a place as any to start it with the wheels, front first. Strip it completely. Remove the tyre and tube, brake assembly and bearings, and wash out all the old grease from the hub with paraffin. Next, check the tracks of the bearing for any sign of pitting or wear and before replacing them apply just a couple of drops of 'moly' (molybdenum disulphide lubricant) to the track which will be all the lubricant required for several races. On no account should normal grease be used, as under the continuous heavy braking required under racing conditions, the heat generated will melt it, and some may well find its way on to the shoes, which are best scrapped should this occur. When you progress to longer distance events you will probably choose to use just enough high melting point grease.

With bearings and spindle replaced and no apparent 'shake' at the spindle, clamp the spindle in a vice, or the fork legs, and spin the wheel to check the truth of the rim. The rim should not be more than 1/8in out of true - maximum. While you are at it also check the tension of every single spoke and they should all 'ring' with about the same note. Before replacing the rim tape that covers the ends of the spokes, check that there are no sharp ends that could pierce the the tape and puncture the tube. File them down as necessary.

Now for the brake. The standard shoes may well have served quite satisfactorily on the road. They may even suffice for the first few ventures into racing, but they will certainly be called upon to do a lot more work than ever before. In dissipating the heat generated by heavy braking, it could well be that the material from which the touring linings are made is inadequate to cope and will 'glaze', to the considerable detriment of the braking effect. Hence the reasons for fitting racing linings. If you choose to do this the type required is the Ferodo grade RM2 or AM4 material. With new shoes fitted make sure that all the lining bears on the brake drum, it will need bedding down before the best effect is obtained.

Here, it is worth noting that the regulations do allow the fitting of different materials to the brake shoes - in the interests of safety. They also permit the fitting of air scoops to the brakes to assist in removing the unwanted heat. If you are fitting a new scoop, or extending an old one, make sure that there is a piece of gauze at the entrance to prevent water getting in, or you will have less brakes not more, when it rains.

Security bolts

Now before we get around to fitting tyre and tube, one more chore. Fitting a security bolt. Without one to clamp the tyre to the rim it is possible for the tyre to turn on the rim under braking stresses. Some competition alloy rims have serations in the 'well' to provide a grip for the tyre while those fitted by Dunlop racing service will be held in place by small screws through the rim that just pierce the tyre. Whether you intend to use the tube and tyre that you already have, one thing's certain - that the tube must have no patches in it. These could well lift when the tyre gets hot - and it will. The tyre itself need not be of the racing pattern. In fact many racers use the excellent Dunlop TT100 tyre both front and back and they will provide all the adhesion that you can use for a long time.

Wheel balancing

Even with the tyre fitted and running dead true there is still one operation to be carried out, and that is the all important balancing job. An out of balance wheel can ruin a machine's roadholding. To do it, set the wheel up so that it is free to revolve, then it will stop with the heaviest point at the bottom and weights are added to the spoke opposite until there is no one particular point heavier than any other. The weights may be purchased from any Triumph dealer as they are a standard Triumph part. The alternative is lead wire wound around the appropriate spoke.

The drill for the rear wheel is almost identical, with a few exceptions: The grade of the brake linings recommended is the slightly softer RM2 material and an air scoop on the rear wheel is of doubtful value. Two security bolts are frequently fitted since the acceleration stresses have also to be catered for. Fit them at 120° with respect to the valve. Lastly, on both wheels, make sure that a valve cap is fitted. The scrutineer should pick you up if you don't have these vital items fitted, because at racing speeds centrifugal force could lift the Schrader valve from its seat causing sudden tyre deflation. That is unless a valve cap is fitted.

With at least the wheels in a raceworthy condition we turn to the suspension that controls their movements, and is therefore a prime factor in a machine's roadholding.

Front forks

When a machine leaves the factory the suspension is intended to cope with the widest possible variations in loadings. From carrying say two passengers totalling 25 stone, plus maybe panniers and luggage. It's not unreasonable to assume that spring rates and damping characteristics can be changed with advantage in racing circumstances.

This operation, like the many other operations described, while beneficial, is not essential to trying your hand at the game. Even if the bike does not steer as well as the other machines, and the chances are that it won't, it won't stop you at least having a provisional gallop.

Having decided that experimentation is worthwhile and bearing in mind the comments on the spring ratings with which it left the factory, a lighter spring should be tried first. The damping can work to better effect in controlling the suspension's movements if it has lighter springs, but the overriding factor here can be the grade of oil that is used as the damping medium. This is in any case affected by the temperature on the day but I am talking of the range from a chilly October meeting to the height of summer which could give a variation of 40°. A thicker grade of oil for the hot weather and perhaps a 20 grade for winter. It's not that critical though, but nevertheless a significant factor.

From those few pointers on the spring ratings and oil grades we seem to have missed a few checks en-route. We have made the assumption that the forks are in good condition with no unscheduled play in any of the moving parts. However, a neglected component is the steering head race bearings and the condition and adjustment of these can make all the difference. The forks must be just free enough to turn under their own weight as they pass over centre point.

Rear suspension

From the front of the machine to the rear. First check the wheel for sideways movement - which could denote a worn wheel bearing, but since this check should already have been made it will show up swinging arm bearings that require servicing. Here it's worth pointing out that if you don't detect a

Fig. 5 — Paul Smart is one of the real stars of the '70s. His way out 'climb off it' style has earned him works rides for Triumph, Kawasaki and Ducati. He has scored notable victories on all three makes but really arrived when winning the 1972 Imola 200 Miler on a Ducati vee twin 750 and his rides on the Team Hanson Kawasaki bikes, 100 bhp three cylinder two strokes.

deficiency here the scrutineer will, because this is one routine check that is usually made by him at every meeting.

On to the rear suspension units. British ones, at least the Girling type in use on most later machines, are sealed and cannot be experimented with; some foreign ones however can be drained and refitted with other oils. The comments on oil grades applied to the forks apply equally if you have the chance to experiment. Also the springs may be changed with advantage, they could be as good as possible with the standard items, you may think the roadholding excellent anyway, but almost any model can be improved.

Another avenue for experimentation lies in the adjustability of most units - two or three positions incorporated originally intended to cope with the varying loads imposed by one and two-up riding. Try the bike on the soft setting first and work upwards.

A point in connection with the regulations here is that at the time of writing it was permissible to change the spring units for other types as you choose. A popular move here is that of fitting Girling units to foreign machines to improve roadholding. A letter to Girling's competition department at this time and they will advise on the spring poundage to fit. That is as long as you supply full details of machine and rider weights.

General Cycle preparation

A frequently neglected item here is the control cables. Having previously paid particular attention to the front brake it's not much good having a cable that is going to let you down. Your neck could depend on its being 101% perfect. If in doubt get a new one and it might be worth searching for a proprietary item with a thicker inner as a little insurance, it also cuts out a little sponginess in some brake actions and if you can find a cable with a nylon inner lining so much the better to add to the smoothness and sensitivity of action. The regulations say nothing against changing these. The same comments apply equally to clutch cables and rear brake cables if any.

It is permissible to alter riding positions and controls to suit the driver's preference and some machines are supplied with the control pedals reversed, compared with British machines. Here it is frequently possible to obtain the parts necessary to swap the pedals over to the other side of the bike and dealers specialising in racing these makes of machine usually stock a conversion if you require British positioning. An important aspect of machine preparation is that of positioning all the controls to that everything falls naturally to hand when assuming a racing crouch. The whole idea of course is to streamline the rider to the machine to reduce wind resistance and improve performance. There are many rearset footrest kits on the market to help achieve the required crouch but the one thing that they will do that will be necessary for racing is to provide greater ground clearance for cornering angles that will certainly exceed any normally used on the road.

Clip-ons

Rearset footrests are normally complemented by 'drop' bars or clip-ons. However, a point to bear in mind here with regard to the regulations is that you can only use the clip-on type bars if they are listed by the manufacturer as an 'optional extra'. Otherwise the rules require the original mounting of the handlebars to be retained, though the shape may be varied. There are many types of proprietary bars on the market to give a lower riding position and the choice of a suitable model may well be decided by whether they will also give sufficient clearance on full-lock to avoid knocking on the petrol tank and trapping your fingers and thumbs. The scrutineer will check this during examination and will reject the bike if it does not give plenty of clearance between the bars and control levers and any other part of the machine, the fairing for instance. This requirement can be difficult to comply with and may need adjustment or modification to the 'stops' that prevent the wheel turning beyond a certain point. It is often possible to fit some packing to achieve the required clearances.

Fairings are an item that may be fitted if you wish. The particular hazard in this respect is that of ground clearance. Today's tyres provide so much adhesion that under racing conditions it is actually the engines that are touching the track on some machines. You may not reach this stage initially, or ever, but it does demonstrate the difference between riding on the public roads and that of competition work.

Ground clearance brings up the subject of exhaust pipes and silencers, because these seem to be the things that touch first, and anything like that could create problems when you have plenty else to think about. The regulations do permit you to alter the positioning of these items to create more cornering clearance although the diameter of the pipe must remain the same and the type of silencer must not change, nor its shape. One exception here that is allowed is the Triumph track silencer, commonly referred to as the 'Thruxton' silencer. Apart from needing the extra ground clearance here, continually scraping pipes and silencers will, not surprisingly, wear holes in them to the detriment of their silencing efficiency. Anyway, scrutineers will probably reject a machine with holed silencers, both for the lack of silence and because the bike will be in a dangerous condition.

Petrol tanks are another item that can create problems. There are many very racy models in the accessory shops that add something to the appearance of a bike but you cannot fit any one you fancy. Once more it is the item that is listed by the manufacturer that can be used. Some do list alternative capacity models and they are practically essential for the longer races where maximum distance is required between refuelling stops.

After all the don'ts and can'ts of the previous paragraphs it's refreshing to find a component over which you have a free choice. If you want to fit a racing seat do so by all means. However, while there can be advantages in fitting one, particularly on a fast bumpy circuit like the Isle of Man, it's an item that I have been quite happy to do without on short circuits, and you'll have expense enough without unnecessary items.

Mudguards should remain unchanged. But they are items that are prone to give some trouble under racing conditions and particular care needs to be taken to stop them splitting due to vibration. They usually split because they are fitted under stress due to production tolerances between guard and frame. Carefully aligning the holes should cut down chances of failure.

Lighting

The last item for consideration is the lighting. Lights must be in full working order, which means you could get picked up if you suffer a lamp failure just before scrutineering. Charging systems should be fully operational and the scrutineer may well require the engine to be run while he notes that the ammeter shows a charge. One exception to this rule is the rear light assembly which must be removed in the interests of safety.

If a fairing is fitted the headlamp is going to be covered by the front number-plate, but in any case the lamp glass should be covered over with adhesive tape or similar to prevent the glass scattering over the track in the event of a spill.

Racing numbers

On the subject of competition numbers, the stick-on backgrounds, or plates themselves, should be elliptical in shape and 11ins wide by nine high. The numbers six inches high and at least one inch in width. With a fairing the mounting is easy, otherwise a good material to use for the plates is hardboard. The adhesive numbers may be bought, or if you buy Fablon and cut them out yourself it works out cheaper. Cheapest of all though is to paint them on but it hardly seems worth the trouble. Numbers and backgrounds must be matt non-reflective, or the sun shining across them will make them difficult to read for the timekeepers, which could mean that they miss you and you don't figure in the results after all your hard work.

Another point about numbers is that the colours vary with the different capacity classes. For a start all front plates are black on white. But for the sides it goes like this: Up to 250, white numbers on a green background; up to 500, black on yellow; up to 1,000, black on white.

When racing, everything is subject to far more stress than it normally gets. Vibration from an engine revving higher for longer periods than before will loosen nuts and bolts that never ever came loose before, and since just one loose nut could cost you a race it's well worth taking the trouble over each and every nut to make sure it stays put.

If your bike has a front wheel stand come mudgaurd stay like the Triumph you may well be requested by the scrutineer to wire it up to make quite sure it does not loosen. Drilling a small hole through the nut, passing a strand of copper wire through the hole and twisting the ends about the nearest lug or tube is the most secure method of ensuring that it does not come undone and this is worth doing on almost every nut that secures something important. An alternative is Loctite, a fluid marketed by Triumph among others, which when applied to threads sets hard and effectively prevents any inadvertent loosening. One more method is to use nuts with nylon inserts in the threads, these act by virtue of the friction imposed by the nylon as a locking device.

To be removed

After telling you about some of the things that you can add and modify, there are those that must be removed as required by the regulations. First of these is the centre-stand. This is certain to ground when you lay the bike right over and that is why it must be removed. Also the side stand for the same reason, some of those could touch and be a nuisance. More important, they could fetch you off and bring down a following rider and cause a multiple tangle.

Other items to be removed are any luggage carriers, pannier frames, etc, club badges, crash bars and licence holders. Anything that could be dangerous if in a spill. One last item, the control levers. You may have noticed bikes with ball-ended levers - this is so that the sharp ends cannot cause injury. Ball-ended levers are obligatory for this reason. In the TT in 1972 they even wanted ball-ended footrests under the rubbers.

The motor

There are no short cuts in motor tuning. No magical formula for instant power. These pages are not intended to be a substitute for other works which seek to modify motors for maximum performance. The basic aim here shall be the achievement of reliability first, because unless you can get a few races in without major trouble you are unlikely to gain the experience from which you will do your own preparation, without reference to books. Experience gained in actual competition is worth all the volumes on the subject and this will in turn teach you what items are particularly important on your own model, and its strengths and weaknesses.

You will no doubt have driven the bike hard enough on the road before acquiring the desire to try your hand at racing. It goes without saying that you will approach the subject with some preconceived ideas. But it's unlikely that you will ever have used the bike so hard before, and with all the extra stresses that racing imposes the motor will have to suffer. So unless you think you can restrain your right hand sufficiently, or are willing to gamble that your motor is unburstable, consider renewing every part that has already served you well, particularly with regard to highly stressed items like drive and timing chains.

Is it worn?

How many miles the bike has done on the road will probably be the best guide as to what parts to renew. It's practically impossible to tell with certainty just how much wear may have taken place on vital bearings until you strip the motor and check the tolerances properly. Do strip the motor right down and start from scratch. You'll probably end up doing it yourself anyway once you are racing regularly. Or at least if you are in doubt as to your ability, take the motor out of the frame, strip it as far as you feel confident, perhaps the head and barrel, and take the rest to a reputable dealer, preferably one with a good reputation for racing preparation, and have him check it for you.

Now while the crankcase is apart it is the time to consider the fitting of any alternative parts that may be listed for your model. Things like high performance camshafts or close ratio gears. However it's much better to get a standard motor

Fig. 6 — Jeff Webber's 500 cc Honda four. There are only currently two or three of these competing. The most notable is that of Bill Smith who won the class at Silverstone and finished third in the TT but that particular model does seem faster than most of its kind.

running properly rather than fit every listed high performance part and spend the first six meetings trying to get all the settings right while you get blown-off by the man with the standard lot who still has the money for the extra parts in his pocket. It happens, and more often than you'd think.

Close ratio gears

Close ratio gears are a definite advantage for racing, you are hardly ever likely to require a bottom gear as low as the standard one, and if on the odd occasion you do, the gap between it and the next ratio will be embarrassingly wide. If you can afford them they are worthwhile but since they can be detrimental to the bike's performance in traffic, if you have to continue using it on the road, perhaps wait until you've decided you are really converted.

This too is the time to consider whether a rebalancing operation is desirable on the crankshaft. Many machines have a vibration period at some place in the rev range. If it occurs when using it on the road you will probably not have to worry as on the track the motor should be running at revs above this. If it is at the top of the range though it's better to get the balance factor checked by a professional oefore reassembly. Balancing factor? The weight of the various reciprocating parts, a certain percentage of which is counter-weighted on the crankshaft by means of the flywheels and bob weights. This may be altered by removing metal from the various parts to increase or decrease the percentage, effectively moving the vibration period up or down the rev range. Again it's a job for a professional if you are not too sure.

The information you require to check all the tolerances will be contained in the manufacturer's workshop manual. A normal maintenance manual is useless for these operations and the £1.50 or so that you may have to spend to obtain a workshop manual - you may have to write direct to the manufacturer or concessionaire - will be worth its weight in gold when you have nobody to turn to. The chief instruments that you will require for the checking operation are a two inch micrometer and a set of feeler gauges.

With all bearings in perfect order and all oilways and parts scrupulously clean, complete the assembly of the bottom half of the engine. Oil pumps are every bit as important as the other vital components, so make sure the pump's perfect.

Cylinder barrels are next on the agenda and the check for wear here, as all the good books will tell you, is whether there is any detectable step between the part of the bore where the piston rings do not touch - and where they do. For touring it's permissible within limits but for racing it's out. Better to get the ridge honed out, or rebore the barrel if it's too far gone.

Compression ratio

One thing that the regulations almost encourage is the raising of compression ratios. They go so far as to say that this may be done. If you are fitting new high compression pistons it's as well to check the clearances between the piston at top dead centre and the valve head, when the valve is in the fully open position. There is usually sufficient between the deepest part of the cutaway in the piston to accommodate it, but it's not unknown for the valve to just clip the edge of the recess, which will then require some metal to be removed from the piston. Personally I like to have about .040 between the piston and valve as a little insurance against valve and piston touching if you miss a gear at high revs. The results can be a bent valve at best and a major blow-up at worst.

The cylinder head

There is always much talk in racing circles about opening out ports, bigger carburetters, lightening valve gear and so on. At first it's best to forget it all but later you'll probably want to have a go. For a start oversize carburetters and valves are forbidden by the regulations. Valves may only be changed if the list of alternative parts for your model shows them to be listed. Optional extra carbs are banned for production racing even if they are specifically listed. Which leaves port shaping. It's so easy to remove metal from the wrong part of a port, to the detriment of the smooth flow of the column of gas trying to get in, that it's best left alone unless you are quite sure what you are doing. The best thing is to merely remove all surface irregularities in the port and leave the shape alone. Don't even bother to obtain a polish to the surface, it's worth is negligible.

This is not to say that nobody but a manufacturer can improve a cylinder head. There are tuners about, who for a sum will 'gas flow' one for you, but by the time you are ready to use the few extra mph resulting you will probably have an idea what it means - other than just a specialised method of obtaining the best shape of port.

For four-stroke owners lightening rocker gear can be a source of happy hours spent removing metal yourself from the rocker arms, push-rods, valve caps, valves, etc. or you may choose to pay to have it done for you. Beware, only remove metal from an obviously unstressed portion of a component - the tips of a rocker arm for instance - you could unknowingly weaken it. It is however a reasonable idea to remove the surface casting irregularities and polish. A polished surface is less likely to lead to cracks that a production machining mark may initiate.

With the cylinder head in place, one can gain or lose a little when replacing the carbs. Ideally of course the inlet port should blend perfectly with the carburetter. It matters less if there is a step caused by the port being slightly larger in places due to its not being entirely round than if there is a step the other way round, when there will actually be an obstruction presented to the incoming gases. The necessary metal should be removed with a fine file and the marks cleaned up with fine emery cloth.

An item that may be removed to improve performance, if you so choose, is the air filter. Having done so you might try fitting a main jet at least one size larger since, with more air flowing in, now that some restriction has been removed, more fuel is required to restore the correct mixture proportions.

Ignition timing

With the previous few hints on motor preparation the job is largely complete. A word about ignition timing though, since this has a vital effect upon the maximum performance. It's not possible to give a general guide in terms of a figure to suit all machines since it varies from say 28° before top dead centre fully advanced for a 750cc Dunstall Norton, to 40° for a Triumph Bonneville with a 10½ : 1 compression ratio.

Setting the timing is simple enough, like most things, when you know how. Where it is possible, use a timing light, a so-called stroboscope, to check the setting. Most dealers use them now and in any case they are generally used on cars and cheap kits for doing it yourself are in car accessory shops. You can of course always have your local shop set it up for you, as long as they have a light, but this is not to say that you cannot get the setting spot-on yourself by normal 'static' means - you can if you take the time and trouble. The light method merely confirms that the timing is correct with the motor actually running.

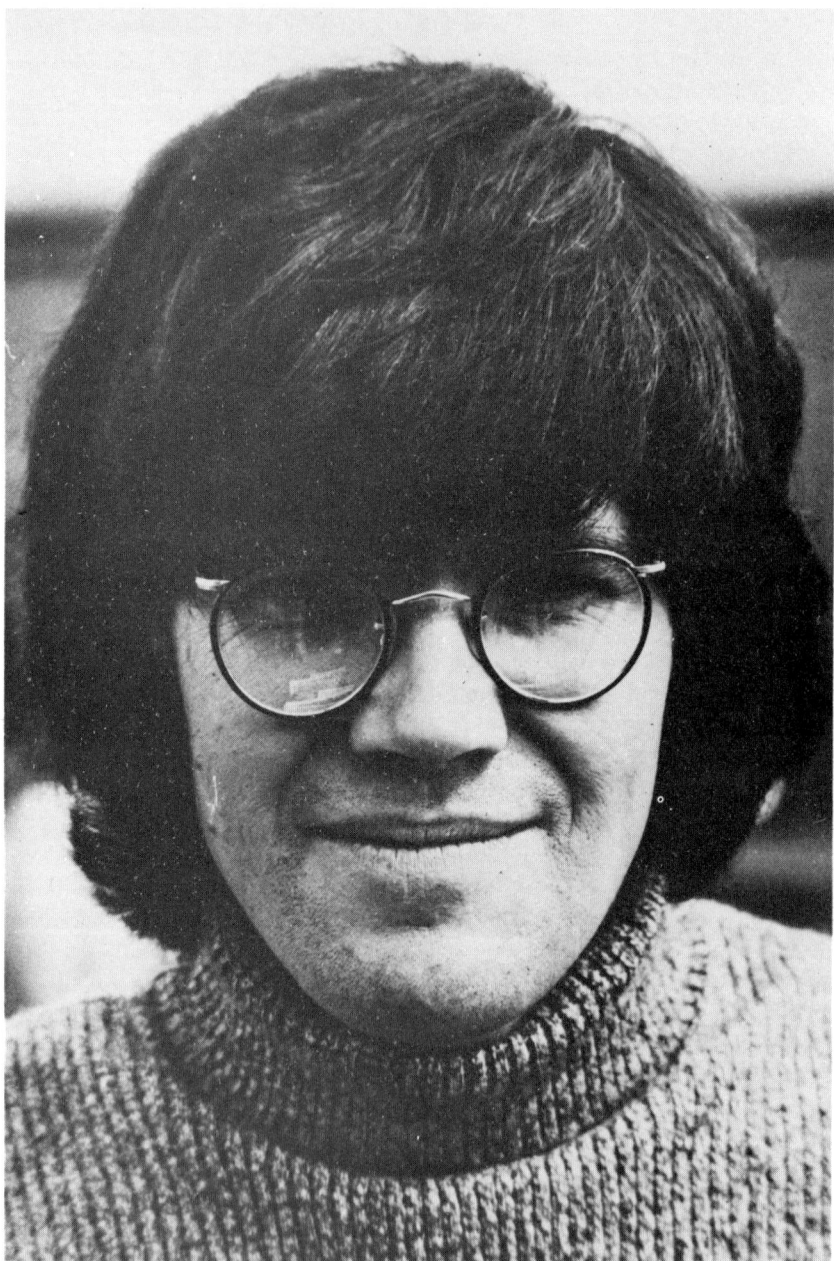

Fig. 7 — Peter Williams is Norton's development engineer works rider par excellance. A rare combination of accomplished rider and first class engineer he is responsible for much of the performance of the Commando and the racing John Player Nortons. He was second in the TT in '72 on a Commando and gets one round the Island at over 100 mph.

Chapter 6
What to race

You may well not have much choice when it comes to a model with which to make your production racing debut. Like me when I started, the bike that took me to work every day, on holiday and everywhere else, had also to serve as a racer. This is the one thing that production racing has to offer, the chance to sample the 'hard stuff' without having to buy a special machine for the job, and one that you can't use for anything but racing either. If you decide racing is not for you then you have to sell the bike at a sizeable loss. If you buy a production bike to go racing with and change your mind you can at least use it on the road.

If you are in the happy position of being able to buy a bike to go racing with, then the choice of capacity class is a serious one, but so often the choice is already made depending on the model that you already have. Whether you are buying a bike especially for the job or using your roadster for a tryout - a few words on the subject of choice.

A well prepared 650 or 750 production racing bike is almost as fast - or even faster - than some of the stripped and tuned to the utmost 1,000cc class racing machines. As such, you will require a fair amount of skill and nerve to use one to its full potential. Just to make the point, a 750 Triumph Trident has lapped the Isle of Man TT course at over 100mph and been clocked at 140mph plus, to illustrate the performance that may be got from a bike equipped with lights and silencers. Admittedly it was a factory machine and yours is unlikely to be anywhere near as quick but it takes an exotic, multi-cylindered one-off special racing bike that money cannot buy, with Hailwood or Agostini aboard, to get round the same course at 107/108mph.

The over 500cc class is certainly the most competitive and glamorous, however, if you are first past the chequered flag everybody knows and you will most probably see it reported in the press too. But the 500s and 250s race every bit as hard, and spend all their cash on their bikes which makes it seem a bit unfair when they seldom get a mention for a class win and rarely achieve the same kind of news as the bigger bangers. The two possible exceptions though are the TT, where there is actually an interval start for the classes, and the 500 Mile Race when it does carry some weight. But in a club race it's the overall winner that gets most of the glory.

Having raced, and won, in all classes I must confess that there is something about being the first bike home in spite of the fact that I've had some great dices on a 500. The 1,000cc class is certainly the most competitive and success in this class usually means that you are the one that is noticed if there is anyone there to see, and if there is, there just might be a faint chance of finding yourself a sponsor - and it is a faint chance believe me, but you never know.

The bigger the bike the faster you'll expect to go and the faster you go the more skill you will need to use it properly. There are a lot more competitors in this class too and generally speaking the bikes are a lot dearer. As well as the bikes being dearer the bigger they are, there is commensurate wear and tear on things like tyres and chains, also since there are more competitors in the big class there are likely to be more riders that can use one to good effect, so all-in-all you really put yourself up against it with a big bike. In short if you feel you really have the ability and want to make your mark in as short a time as possible then the big class is for you.

Disillusion comes very hard and it's never a bad thing to learn to walk before you can run, start at the bottom and work upwards. The 250cc class has a lot to commend it. After all you start off on one on the roads and are unlikely to be embarrassed with an overabundance of power at a time when you have so many other things to concentrate on. A 250 can be very inexpensive to run, comparatively of course, as no racing is cheap. Roadholding on a smaller bike should, all things being equal, be better than on a larger model; you are not as likely to be underbraked as some of the bigger bikes are and when you can really drive hard you will be able to corner faster on a smaller bike than a larger one and when you do move up the capacity scale the experience will stand you in very good stead.

True at the present time all capacities are in the same race and you are likely to have the big bikes around at the same time, but there are likely to be other beginners around with whom you can dice. When you do start getting the hang of things anyway, you may well find yourself burning off some of the bigger bikes and there is very great satisfaction in that. Almost as much as winning outright.

Hardware

Now to tackle the hardware, smallest class first. There is plenty of variety available in power units from single cylinder four-strokes to three cylinder two-strokes. But to take a successful and simple model first, the Ducati. Its single overhead camshaft engine is particularly robust and ideal for a start in club racing since with little modification it's quite quick enough to get you a class win. One particular tip I can offer for this model is to be meticulous about changing the oil frequently when you are racing it since the oil capacity is only four pints.

Later versions of the Ducati have what they call 'desmodromic' valve gear. This is just a very technical sounding phrase for having the valves opened and closed mechanically rather than being closed by valve springs. Springs absorb quite a significant proportion of engine power which is a good reason for this development, but even better is that the arrangement permits better valve control and higher revolutions. Naturally this version is faster than the old one and this bike ridden by Charles Mortimer won its class in the TT in 1970.

The other four-stroke worth mentioning is the Honda twin cylinder overhead camshaft model with its five speed gearbox, though at a quoted 353lbs its 30bhp at 10,500rpm has plenty to do. The latest version of this is certainly fast and it won in 1971 and 1972.

Other available models are the BSA/Triumph 250 single cylinder ohv models, but these with their old fashioned design stand little chance of being competitive against the faster foreign contenders. The now obsolete Royal Enfield Crusader suffers from the same disadvantages but they could provide a start.

Of the choice of two-stroke models available the Suzuki seems to be very popular in club circles. Its six speed gearbox gives excellent acceleration and it has put in some fine performances in recent 500 Mile Races, winning its class three times and finishing second overall on one occasion.

The Spanish Ossa machine is a bit of an enigma in that it is particularly fast. Indeed it has a TT win to its credit, yet it is seemingly not popular in club racing circles as I've yet to see one about apart from the International events in which it is entered by the British concessionaires.

The Yamaha is becoming increasingly popular in club racing. Straight out of the crate, almost, it seems to go well and indeed in 1971 and 2 came home second in its class in the TT. Latest in the class is the three cylinder Kawasaki but at the time of writing it was still too new to have showed its potential. The older twin cylinder model while quite quick on the road has never really figured in the results on the track.

Fig. 8 — The author on his own 'bought paid for and tuned Trident. The bike has the Fontana front brake and Quaife five speed close ratio gear cluster. With standard cams and pistons it is capable of about 130 mph in the Isle of Man and holds a club lap record at Snetterton.

Two singles complete the quarter litre capacity class and they are the Bultaco and Montesa. The chief claim to fame of the Bultaco is that one still holds the TT lap record for the class set, back in 1967, at over 89mph, but this was achieved with the use of an expansion chamber type of exhaust system which while permissible in Spain on the roads at the time is no longer allowed in production racing.

The Montesa is probably the cheapest bike you can buy in the class and can be made to go quite well, though I've only seen a couple about. If that concludes the 250 class I might be forgiven for not dealing with all the 350s that you can buy since they have the in-built disadvantage that they have to compete in the 500cc class - it goes from 251 to 500, and you cannot give away 150ccs and really expect to win all things being equal, which in racing they seldom are. So don't be put off by it.

So on to the 500s where you have a wide choice of machinery ranging from singles to fours. To start with the Velocette. This has a real race-bred history with many wins to its credit and the greatest thing to say about it for somebody starting is that the Venom Clubman model is fitted with all the racing extras and is ready to go without having to fit any more parts. Its single cylinder ohv is a design that dates back practically to the year dot, but it could still be made competitive.

Another single is the Ducati 450 desmodromic model of which there have been one or two about in club racing, but as yet they have not yet proved to be appreciably faster than the 250cc model - which is a bit of a mystery.

Another enigmatic machine is the BSA Gold Star pushrod single cylinder OHV model. On paper it should not stand a chance and in club racing it seldom does.

But with scrambles internals fitted it has proved fast enough and reliable enough to have won the FIM Coupe de Endurance series. In the TT in '72 two were timed at 122mph - but they both retired.

The Honda CB500 is the latest four cylinder machine to hit the British scene and Bill Smith rode one to third place in the TT in 1972 but until there is more development carried out its not really quick enough, in showroom condition, to beat the opposition. The Honda CB440 does not seem to command the popularity that it might well in club racing, there have only been one or two about in the last couple of years. But in '69 Graham Penny won the class in the TT on one so it goes without saying that they can be made to go well.

The Suzuki two stroke twin 500 has a couple of TT wins to its credit and can be particularly rapid. It holds the lap record at 93.61mph but it does pose problems on a tight course due to lack of ground clearance between the silencers and the track.

With a claimed 60 brake horse power the Kawasaki three pot stroker should be capable of blowing off all the other 500s but its not quite the case yet. When first introduced the roadholding was diabolical but later models are quite good in standard trim and can certainly be improved easily. Ridden by Hugh Evans in the 1972 TT one was clocked at 124mph, the fastest timed speed for a production 500. We could yet see one in front of the field.

The Triumph Daytona is still one of the most popular 500s in club racing. Its simple motor responds to tuning well and it steers and stops with little alteration.

Its been winning its class in International competition for many years now and will continue to do it in club events for several more seasons yet. Even at an International level its far from finished.

Now for the big class. It's the one that attracts all the glamour and the one in which British manufacturers actively support racing. With a bike that goes well in this class you can easily switch to the 1,000cc racing class on the same machine and give a good account of yourself - if you have the ability.

In International events the capacity limit is 750ccs, though there are indications that one or two manufacturers have larger models on the stocks, so the limit might later be raised to 1,000ccs which it is for all club races. You do in these events get the odd 1,000cc Vincent competing but without a doubt the most successful model around the club scene these days is the Norton Commando Production Racer. This is a model in its own right fitted as it leaves the factory with almost every aid to going faster that you can dream up. Even so its possible to add to that with a five speed gear cluster and twin disc brake assembly but either way it will provide enough performance to win just about anything. But then it is the only model that you can buy (its in very limited supply) as a production racing bike.

The next most popular and until recently about the most successful production bike ever, is the Triumph Bonneville. There are a list of extras for this bike that will make it competitive but even without them its quick enough to continue winning races for many a season yet - if you ride hard enough. My own experience with this model suggests that it can be made extremely rapid but eventually you reach the point where it starts to become unreliable.

The BSA 654cc twin Spitfire model is one with a rather chequered competition history in big class events having been more than competitive on occasion, but dogged by ill-luck or lack of reliability. For club events this machine is certainly capable of winning and indeed has done on many an occasion and no doubt will again. You may wonder why I've left the Triumph/BSA three cylinder models until this far down the list. Well, there are still not many about in racing trim and comparing their standard specification to the Norton Commando Racer they are not likely to come out on top. For a start they are under braked so you would need to fit a disc or Fontana brake to stop in anything like competitive distance. Then close ratio set of four or five speed gears would be a great help.

So you can see that there is work to do, but once its done it will really be in among the Nortons and in fact at an International level it does have a better record in competition.

Dunstall Nortons and Commandos are basically Norton machines but extensively modified by Paul Dunstall who is in fact a registered manufacturer in his own right. He can provide a specification to suit your bank balance and there is little doubting the performance of a machine that has established world's records and won the production TT in 1968. There are not many about the tracks since most of them go to America.

First on the British scene among the big multis from abroad is the Honda CB750. A lot of machine that has never realised the potential on the track that it's specification suggests. There are just a few about the circuits but apart from the odd club win nothing more. There are goodies listed for them but they never seem to be available. Some seem to go quickly in standard trim but others are slow by comparison. If you've got one try it, yours might be quick.

At the time of writing, towards the end of the 1972 season, there had been no sign of the four cylinder Yamaha or indeed of the four stroke twin on the track but the Kawasaki 750 three cylinder two stroke had won its first National production machine race in the hands of John Hedger at Brands Hatch. It appeared in the TT but was obviously so new that its slowness was naturally excusable, being clocked at 122mph. But it goes without saying that they will be about and must have a terrific potential if its low speed torque on the roads is translated to track performance.

The big water cooled Suzuki three is rather like the big Yamaha - with a big question mark to see what it will be like when somebody does get around to racing one and that might also be said of the big BMW's, since apart from what purported to be a couple of privateer entries in the TT nothing has been seen of

Fig. 9 — A rare Kawasaki 750 ridden by John Hedger and entered by Owen Five Star. The tremendous low speed torque of the two-stroke three enabled John to win on this machine at Twisty Brands Hatch but on Silverstone's long straights it did not prove to be particularly fast.

them. Frankly those in the Island did not look to be in the same class as the fastest Nortons or Triumphs.

Laverda are starting to be seen occasionally now and I've even ridden one myself and although quick in that race at Silverstone the bike is intended more as a long distance event machine rather than a short circuit scratching device. It probably lacks a little at the top end of the range.

The big Moto Guzzi vee twin is another that is too new in competition to give a fair assessment of its chances although they do seem to steer particularly well. They have showed well on the Continent, like the Laverda, but have not yet made their British debut.

Another vee twin is the Ducati. Potentially competitive and winners of the Imola 200 Mile Race in Italy, but that was in out and out racing trim for the Formula 750 class but they, like the others should be about soon.

The choice is enormous, limited only by the depth of your pocket, but so is any racing and if it was not limited then you would probably not be considering production racing at all but making an offer for Agostini's M.V. Augusta. In fact production racing could well be far more interesting at National and International level than open class racing in the future.

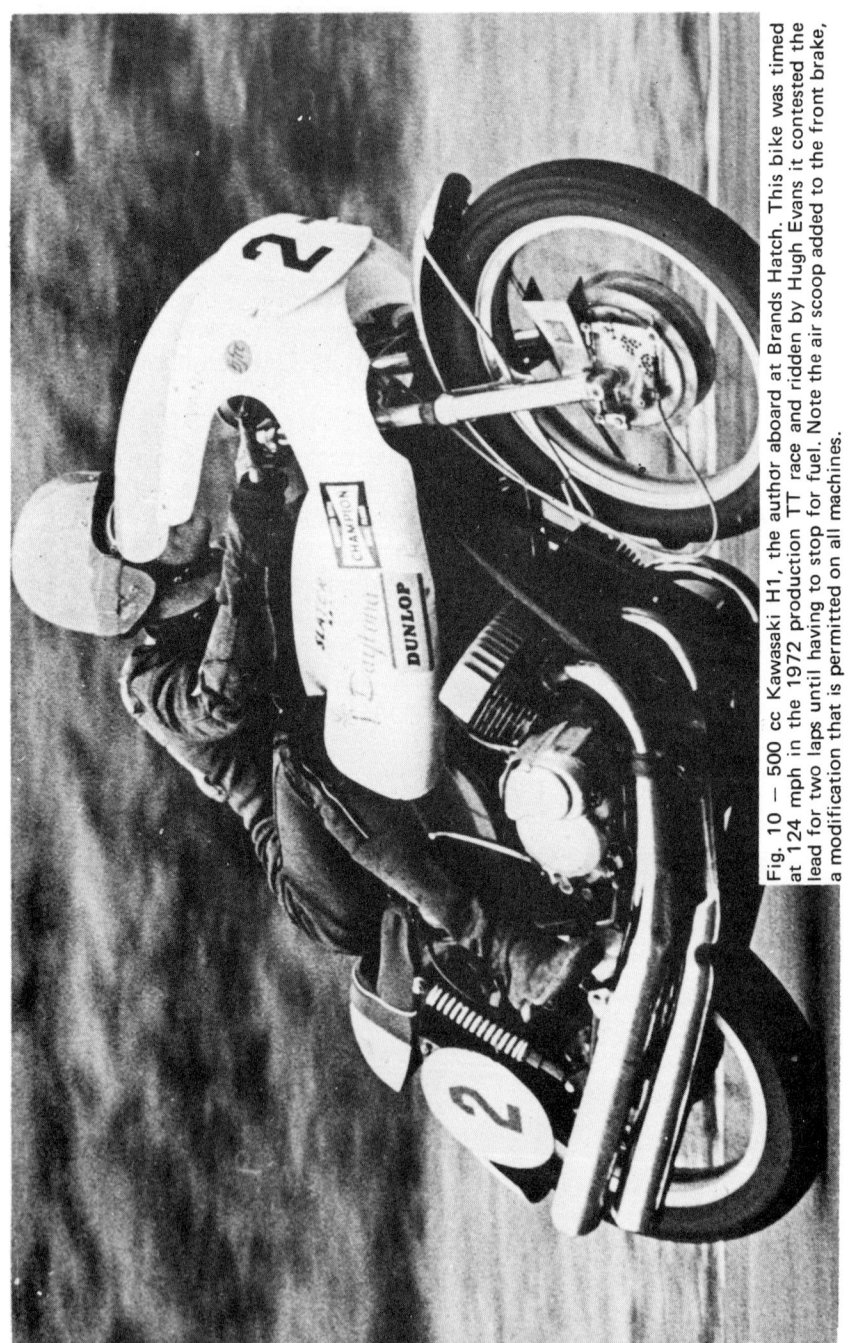

Fig. 10 — 500 cc Kawasaki H1, the author aboard at Brands Hatch. This bike was timed at 124 mph in the 1972 production TT race and ridden by Hugh Evans it contested the lead for two laps until having to stop for fuel. Note the air scoop added to the front brake, a modification that is permitted on all machines.

Chapter 7
Riding techniques

There is no real substitute for sheer ability of the stuff of which champions are made. Some riders can go very quickly with no real effort, others will never make it, but the majority could probably benefit by taking a reasoned approach to their racing - certainly at club level where there is often more enthusiasm than experience, a little science could make you faster, and faster safer.

On paper there is only one fastest line through a corner, the line that makes the greatest radius. The faster you can travel through a corner the faster you will approach the next straight and the quicker you will reach your top speed, whereas the man with a faster bike may actually be slower than you down the straight because he enters it so much slower and before he can reach maximum has to shut off for the next bend. A good rider can often make a slower machine appear much faster to the onlooker than it really is. The old saying that a good rider is a tuner's best gimmick is so true. A good man can be worth several miles per hour down the straight let alone generally outriding the others.

Now I said that the theoretical fastest line through a corner is that which gives the greatest radius, and there's the rub. There are so frequently considerations that alter circumstances, like a series of ripples in the track that upset a machine's roadholding. Avoid them and you get through faster. There may well be another bend immediately following which requires a different point of entry from that in which you will find yourself after getting through the first one, so that it is better to actually go slower through the first one and achieve a faster time through the several corners. Then you may well have to change a line to get around a slower rider. There may well be somebody challenging for your position and attempting to get inside you and force you to take the slower line - it's all in the game, dicing at close quarters is what it's all about. Another way to beat a man on a faster bike, other than just by sticking your neck out round a corner, is to 'get a tow' - slipstream him, that is apart from just getting in his way at the critical moments, but let's adopt a reasoned approach to this chapter by starting at the beginning.

On the grid
A race can be won or lost at the start. Months of work in the garage to extract that last half a brake horsepower will be for nothing if when the flag goes down

the rest of the field streaks away while you are left on the grid still kicking, or pressing the 'go' button.

The first thing to do before you even get to the grid is to go and watch the starter start the other races before yours. Study his action as he raises the flag. Watch how long he holds it aloft before dropping it. Perhaps he does not. Perhaps he is one of those that whips it straight up and down again without a pause. Whatever brand he may be, as long as he is consistent, you will be able to predict just when the flag starts its downward movement, and that's when the race starts. This is not trying to jump the flag. Just to make sure that as soon as that flag starts to move so does your boot on the kickstart crank. Most competitors wait for the flag to move and then start to kick. The time that you can save here is the reaction time that it takes you to detect the flags first twitch and translate this to movement of your leg. While you are doing it the man who is on the ball will have his motor running and have got into gear. When you've got your motor running he is already several yards in front of you, and races are won and lost by a lot less than several yards, so competitive is racing today.

So get on the ball with a starter - for a start. Although this is not much good if your technique is poor. It shouldn't be necessary to leap six feet in the air and descend with a sickening crunch on the crank just because you have an astronomical compression ratio. Just ease the pistons slightly over compression and then give a long kick that follows right through rather than dab it viciously. Find the throttle setting that will give instant start, if necessary mark the twistgrip and rubber to make sure it's in the best place. The main thing is not to get flustered, try first to be deliberate, the speed will follow.

One item that can cause trouble at the start is the folding footrest, the one that folds to clear the kickstarter's travel. It may be tight upon its pivot. Then you will be bombing off the grid, weaving you hope through the others, while trying to kick down the rest before the first corner. It can be hazardous. The alternative is for the rest to be free to fall down when the kickstart has passed it on its travel, which often works well, until the motor fails to go first prod then the chances are that you'll kick again with the rest down and confusion results. Two answers; One is a rest held in the up position by a spring loaded ball and you can buy this type, another is to adjust the rest so that it is stiff to move - but fix an 'L' shaped piece of metal to the underside of the rest so that you can kick this to bring down the rest once you are on the move.

So we are finally on the move and approaching the first corner, and the first thing you do after all that effort to get the bomb going is to slow it down again. Races are won and lost on braking as much as anything else and here the

54

possibilities for the methodic approach are a little greater than some other aspects of the racing game. The results are easily seen too.

On the approach to most corners you will find marker boards that denote distances to the approaching corner. Like 300, 200 and 100. Now instead of waiting until it looks like being as late as you dare before rolling back the grip and slamming on the anchors, pick out one of the marker boards and with each succeeding lap, using the mark that you have set yourself, brake just that little bit later. Eventually you'll have a point fixed in your mind that is as late as is safe for you.

This method will give consistency to your approach to the corners and ensure that you go through them with the same speed every time. Adopting what is, I feel, the more usual method of estimating the line and speed by eye every time the corner comes up, you cannot hope to make a perfect job of it every time. But pick your braking point, get it right, and the rest falls in to line naturally. Perhaps there is not a marker board so a substitute must be found and this often can be a mark on the track surface, a change of colour, a bit of resurfacing. An alternative can often be found on the track verge, a tuft of grass or something.

Now you might think that cornering is what it's all about. Certainly when any-one thinks racing, the mental picture is one of a bike over on it's footrest with the bike all but sliding. Sure it probably provides the greatest challenge, as you get over so far there is that restraining influence inside you that says far enough and no further, and then somebody comes by and you grit your teeth and try and push the limit up a little. But its not just a case of who can lay the bike over the farthest wins the race.

To go back to spectating. When you see a real star man go through a corner he seldom looks as though he's really trying. If you have seen Hailwood in action you will know just what I mean. The action is so smooth and deceptively easy that it looks child's play, until you try it. While I can claim to be no shining example of the classic style it is certainly the one to cultivate, and the lesson to learn from it is that of doing things smoothly and deliberately.

In these days of the short circuit scratch and scramble to be first round the corner, it's so easy to rush into a corner too fast, throw the bike on its side and go on round on the over-run hoping that the engine braking effect will slow you down sufficiently to enable you to scramble round. Sure you can do it time after time and get away with it, but you will never be quite as fast, and certainly as safe, if you 'make haste slowly'. The ideal, and classic method, is to get all

Fig. 11 — Paul Smart demonstrates the style has has earned him fame and big prizes on the Formula 750 cc racing Ducati. The big Ducati has not yet appeared in this country in production racing trim but the 250 model is a popular one in club racing circles and the single cylinder four stroke can hold its own with the multi-cylindered competition.

your braking and gearchanging done while the bike is still upright, peel off at the predetermined point and drive through the corner increasing the throttle opening on the way through feeling for the point at which the wheel starts to slide and feeding on just enough power before the wheel breaks away. As your technique improves so you will end up cogging down while keeping the front brake hard on for the approaching corner and blending in the action of laying the machine over as you let the front anchor off and commencing to open the throttle, progressively, so that by the time the apex of the bend is reached the power is beginning to come on strong. Driving round under power rather than coming in faster on the over-run is a far steadier, and safer approach.

We have reached the point of having started, slowed it down again, and laid it into a bend, but as you might guess that is not the end ot it. What seems on the face of it to be the obvious line to use, 'ain't necessarily so'. Other factors may mean that a modification to what at face value seems to be a slower line, is in fact beneficial. There could easily be a pothole on the chosen line. More likely there will be two or three bumps together which, run over in quick succession, will really upset the machine's roadholding. While you are getting into that bit of a wobble and sorting yourself out, somebody else will take the long way round and ear'ole round the outside leaving you wondering how the hell he's got the nerve. The other situation that I mentioned before is where you have a couple of corners, or more together, and where it pays to use the less obvious line on the first one to set yourself up right for the second or succeeding ones. So think about the best way.

Without a doubt the best thing to do is to walk around the circuit and watch some of the faster men come through the corners, then have a go at their line.

They probably aren't perfect but it will do to get you into the swing of things time enough to try your own lines when you've a little experience.

You wouldn't think that there was much in winding the bike up and accelerating out of a corner. Just bang it wide open and hang on, wait until it stops going in that gear and kick the gearstick. Well the motor won't last too long for one thing, and in any case, more to the point, you might still not be getting the maximum acceleration. How come you might wonder? Well. Suddenly banging the throttle wide open, just like that, is not necessarily the best way to get optimum results. You can easily 'choke' a motor so that it does not pick up quite so cleanly. There's suddenly more mixture there than the motor can cope with at those revs. Depending on the characteristics of your particular motor, and the state of tune, it may pick up far more quickly and cleanly if you open the throttle progressively. Try progressively quick openings as you accelerate out of a corner to find out which is best for your model. As to why the motor will not last long - if you rev it far beyond its safe limits you invite mechanical disaster. Even if a valve does not touch a piston then you will certainly wear everything out that much quicker.

Slipstreaming

'Getting a tow' is a better name for it, and it certainly describes what you are about. You might get caught and passed by a man with a bike just slightly quicker than yours. Don't despair, if you can get really close to his rear number-plate and tight behind him, you will find that you get drawn along behind in the vacuum that nature is trying to create behind that rapidly moving mass of man and machine. The 'tow' can be worth anything up to another five miles per hour on your top speed and done with cunning it is easy to convince the other man that in fact your bike is actually faster than his. As he comes by, nip into his slipstream but - a word of caution - if he already has somebody right behind him you could have a tangle on your hands so don't swerve over unless you are sure that there is a vacant space, nip into his slipstream and you will get drawn up it and right up to his back mudguard.

Now it is possible to use the impetus so gained to actually pull up alongside, your opponent may well think that you then have the edge. It's all good psychology to get him worried. Anyway the time to make your arrival up alongside, is as you are approaching a corner. Then you can try out a war of nerves on your adversary to see who is going to crack first when it comes to banging the anchors on. But remember your braking point - you know the limit of your brakes. You can either be secure in the knowledge that if he brakes before your marker then you have him beat, or if he outbrakes you and still gets round the bend then either you calculated wrong, or his brakes really are better than yours.

Assume that you have both brakes together and are side-by-side into the corner, make sure that you have the inside line. Because for a start it is the shortest route round the corner and if you do happen to drift a bit wider than you intended then you have still a couple of feet as a safety margin, whereas he will have to let you go if you do use all the road. Now don't assume that this is the object in view because if you do pinch his intended piece of road intentionally then you are riding a spoiling sort of race and being obstructive, and you will soon get unpopular doing that. Not to say that it isn't done but it's more suited to the real cut and thrust up among the professionals at a National meeting.

However the situation will arise so there is a point in mentioning it. But unless you really know your opponent and his riding, and he yours, leave what could turn in to dangerous driving until you have lots of experience when the company you are in will expect it, and because they do, will not cause 'a situation'.

So pick the inside lane, it's safer, if you have to try and drive round the outside of somebody you can now appreciate that they can miscalculate, and if they do and run out of road in the process they could take you with them. Also if you are going round the outside you will naturally have to go that little bit faster, so of course you must be sticking your neck out just a little further. Now it's all very well to pick that fastest line through a corner and set yourself up just right but you can so easily find your line blocked by a slower rider, and short of ramming him up the rear numberplate you have got to either cram on the brakes or swerve round him and find an alternative line. So now the fastest line may well be the most peculiar that you have tried, certainly it will be if there are several riders bunched up in the way. So it pays to know what the results are from taking devious routes sometimes, and know the surface of the track off the accustomed line, it could win you a race someday.

I mentioned that rushing into a corner on the over-run using the motor to provide the last bit of braking was not the desired method of taking a corner, since it leaves no safety margin and you could well end up by coming out of the corner slower as a result anyway. Well the situation happens when you try outbraking somebody when you are really dicing on the limit, and if you can only get in front at that corner then you could well win the race, and after all that is the general idea. With the last corner before the checkered flag, getting in to the bend first can mean everything, in which case you may well find that the calculated risk is worth it, after all if you get in first he has to get round you to beat you to the flag so you are bound to try it sometime but as I've said I don't believe it's the quickest way through a corner, but on occasion it can pay off.

When you get around to taking to the track for the first time, the first thing that will seem strange is finding other riders in such close company, but it is a thing that you will get used to - or retire straight away. You will get other riders diving under your elbow just as you are setting yourself up to take a bend - and it can be a bit unnerving until you are used to it, or fast enough for it not to happen. There will be the time when as you are going in to a corner a faster man comes by and the temptation is to try sitting on his tail and following him round. Don't - you could end up in lots of trouble. His limit might be far greater than yours and you will find yourself travelling at a speed that you will regret. Find your own way round in your own good time, not in the ambulance afterwards.

Fig. 12 — An unusual machine in British tracks is the Laverda 743 cc twin ridden here by Jeff Wade — No. 183 — and entered by the importer, Roger Slater. On the inside is the Commando of Clive Wall on the R.H. Smith sponsored machine. This is a particularly fast version of the 'as you can buy' production racing Norton, having been timed at 133 mph.

A word about the moments before a race. Firstly in the marshaling area. No matter how much space there seems to be, all the competitors seem to congregate around the same spot and this can often lead to the situation where you are practically breathing somebody's exhaust gas as everyone keeps the motors running to get them to the desired warm temperature for the race. So there you are right in the middle of the crowd breathing great gulps of carbon monoxide and surrounded by motors revving. Well if you are new to the game it can't be conducive to calm nerves and concentration to the 'enth' degree that will follow shortly. It doesn't matter if everyone else does think that 'somebody didn't tell you', move out of the madhouse and get a breath of fresh air, it might even calm the butterflies.

Having got yourself out on the grid and in the place that you 'drew out of the hat', you will probably have a wait of several minutes in front of you. Probably the breakdown wagon has still to collect the mechanical casualties from the last race. It's probably the travelling marshal that everybody is waiting for, as until he completes a circuit and reports the track clear another race cannot start. So there you are, as nervous as hell, waiting for things to get started. You can see characters as soon as they get on the grid, foot poised to kick, but the starter is probably not even on his rostrum - and make sure you know exactly where that is and that you can see him clearly. Don't start tickling the carbs in readiness, if your model starts best with a priming that is - you'll probably have the motor flooded if you do. Just 'free' the clutch, switch off the ignition sit back and wait. Even try to find the time to pass a joke with the nearest competitor. You could demoralise him and if you end up dicing with him it could give you just a small psychological advantage. But don't get too blasé, when the starter has the flag in his hand and walks towards the rostrum, then get yourself set to go. After all, you will want to check that the ignition and both petrol taps really are on - for the fourteenth time that is.

About the last few words on riding are devoted to flags. Flags control racing, they are the communication between track officials and the riders and are displayed for every good reasons. The start of the race, and that's a good enough reason, Union Jack of course. To indicate that you have won, you hope, and of course that one is the chequered flag. Then the flag that you must have also seen the yellow - danger flag. It's to warn you of a hazard round the corner, it may even by a partially blocked track with somebody lying in the road - or the bike, then the flag will be waved at you vigorously - great danger. You ignore either, not just at your own peril, which is stupid enough, but you may endanger marshals who may be trying to drag something out of your path. The trouble is that somebody always seems to think that they can stop on the proverbial tanner and go by you, taking advantage of the caution. Apart from the fact that it's not worth it, an erring competitor could be reported by a marshal, and when he is hauled before the Clerk of the Course - or even the ACU Steward, it could cost him races in the future as a penalty.

Another flag that you will see soon anough, and is sometimes the only one that some racers will take notice of is the yellow and red striped one. You'll remember because it means oil on the track, and probably that cement dust has been scattered on it to dry it up, that can be disconcerting too, though it's not as slippery as you think. Then there is the white flag, and hope you don't see it because it stands for an ambulance being on the circuit - and it might be in the middle of the road round the next corner.

Only two more: The red one means stop everything immediately, the race is stopped. There is probably somebody badly hurt laying in the road. The other is green to indicate that the track is clear. Used after a spill to tell you that the track is now clear, or at the beginning of practice to indicate where the signalling points are. They are all meant to tell you something for your own good so watch for them.

Racing success is dependent even more, if possible, upon one's mental and physical attributes than it is upon the competitiveness of the machine. A rider without the qualities to cope with speed and the close competition of short circuit racing could not win on the fastest bike, but on the slowest machine a gifted man would be far from last.

Much is made of the quality of a star rider's speed of reactions and it is frequently assumed that this quality is paramount and that without it you have little hope of success. I don't subscribe to this belief. Reactions certainly play their part in success in the hurly burly of short circuit racing where an opportunity seized brings the winners laurels or avoidance of a 'tangle' when another competitor miscalculates. But it can play little part in making the fastest lap in a race when you are in the happy position of being out in front. The prime quality in that situation is surely pure judgement and as long as one is not of too nervous a disposition this is something that can be developed when you become familiar with re-occurring situations in racing.

Several aquaintances have started racing with no apparent signs of the 'tiger' required to win a race, and yet after a couple of seasons experience developed into fast and consistent riders through acquiring the attitude necessary to go quickly without sticking their necks out. Many of the situations that arise when riding on the road do not occur when racing. In many ways racing can be a lot safer than motorcycling on the open road with all the unpredictable things that can and do happen. When racing you use all the road and there's nobody to come at you from round the next corner. No cars to pull out, or dogs to run across the road. If you do come unstuck then there is somebody at hand to pick you up, and the bike. You will not fall under a lorry and you certainly will be sharing the road with others who are prepared to dodge round you laying in the road, and you will be protected from bruises and grazes by the regulation racing clothing. In case you do hurt yourself, then at least on the track there will be a Doctor readily available to render the necessary treatment.

Indeed, there are far more dangers on the road than the track, that is if you approach the subject with the right mental attitude. If you can ignore the men who are going to rush by you into a corner, and get on with learning the job in hand and feeling out your capabilities, you will learn the craft far quicker in the long run.

The best insurance against being involved in an accidental collision while racing is a style that has predictability. You might well wonder just what that is supposed to mean, and it is in fact that your riding is such that other competitors can, from your position on the track and your attitude on the machine, estimate your intentions and be able to pass you safely.

If you start to run before you can walk and rush into a corner too fast you will probably give yourself a fright and end up running wide and coming out on the grass, if you are lucky enough to have some conveniently situated. A faster man might well have set himself to pass you on that corner but since you are on the 'ragged edge', and therefore somewhat unpredictable, a sudden change of course could be a collision course. Being an experienced man he will probably spot the situation before it arises, at least you hope he will.

Then of course you may approach the corner too slow, 'peel off' too early and end up taking the corner in a series of curves something like the edge of a 50p piece and either generally get in everybody's way or let all your adversaries by. That is just for a straightforward corner, when you get an 'ess' or succeeding corners, as the possibilities for mistakes increase so the chances of gaining an advantage over your fellow competitors also increase, so a little science can be worth several places, a win or avoiding a spill.

Fig. 13 — The ultimate Norton racer of 1972: The Formula 750 machine seen in the paddock at Silverstone and ridden by Phil Read. Much attention has been paid to aerodynamics as may be observed from the shape of the fairing and even the back of the seat is faired to enable rider and machine to blend as one shape with the rider down to it.

Chapter 8
Regulations and specifications

When comparing your 'bog' standard roadster with machines as raced in a production race it will be obvious that much is permitted in the way of changes to machine specifications. Rarely will you see standard 'upright' handlebars fitted to a machine on the track, indeed they are hardly compatible with the aim of the game, achieving a maximum speed greater than that of the opposition. Being stuck up and out into the airstream will out your maximum speed by several miles per hour due to increased wind resistance.

Riding positions laying flat upon the tank can hardly be achieved to the best effect with standard footrests, controls and bars. But it was always possible to fit bars of your choice as long as it did not mean changing the method of mounting. Meaning that you could not just fit the clip-on type of bars normally fitted to racing machinery: These are only permissable if clip-on handlebars are listed by the manufacturer as alternatives to the original specification.

This brings us to just what rules there are on machine alterations and how they are supplied.

Before a machine may be raced its specification must have been lodged by the manufacturer with the Auto Cycle Union, and through it the FIM - the Internation controlling body for the sport, which process when complete is referred to as 'homologation'. When a machine is accepted by the ACU as homologated there will be a complete record of its technical specification and of all the optional extra components that they allow to be fitted for the purposes of production racing.

The ACU make all these details up into a booklet that can be purchased and so you will have a 'logbook' for your bike telling you just what extras you can fit. Perhaps more important, it is possible that a machine examiner at a meeting will ask you to produce it when you attend scrutineering so that he can verify that the bike does conform to the homologated specification and that you therefore have done nothing to contravene the rules. It is indeed placing the onus of proving that the machine conforms to specification upon the competitor and it is incumbent upon the competitor to bring modifications to the notice of the scrutineer. In effect you are guilty until you prove yourself innocent. But

Fig. 14 — The author with 750 Honda in the foreground. (MCI pic).

you need not worry too much at a club meeting as there is seldom time for the searching examinations that are sometimes carried out at International meetings.

Getting back to riding positions. You are allowed to adapt the machine to suit yourself with respect to footrests and controls. This usually means that everyone fits rearset footrests and gearchange and rear brake lever. In the case of machines with gearchange and brake lever reverse from the normal British style, it is possible to fit a crossover conversion to bring the controls to the side that you prefer.

The bars have already been mentioned and even if clip-ons are not listed for your bike then the wide range of bars on the market will surely provide some that give almost the same position as clip-ons. Completeing the racing position, you can fit any type of seat that you wish, which usually means a racing hump backed seat. This is in fact a small aid to positioning yourself on the machine as on a bumby track it will give you something to brace yourself against and make you feel more a part of the machine. But it won't really make very much difference.

Having tailored the riding position to suit your preference another item that you will probably soon want to have a hard look at is the ground clearance. If you took the standard bike straight out onto the track probably the first thing that you would do on the first corner would be to ground the centre stand, side stand or exhaust system, and probably fall off as a consequence. For a start the regulations actually require you to remove the stands as a safety measure because they have in the past caused trouble and brought people off so that is compulsory. After that exhaust pipes and silencers always seem to get in the way when cornering and it can hardly be good for your pocket to wear them out, scraping them on the track until you wear them through, or help the racing by seeing who can slide round on their pipes the fastest. It is therefore permissable to alter the line of the pipe to provide increased ground clearance and this usually means bending pipes or brackets to tuck them in against the frame. Perhaps there are even upswept pipes that can be bought for your model. But you must not alter the diameter of the pipes or put 'flats' on silencers or alter their shape.

The one exception to the silencer situation seems to be what is commonly referred to as the Triumph 'Thruxton' silencers which is accepted in place of the standard item and is homologated extra on the 650s and 500s.

If you have done everything permitted in the last couple of paragraphs then you will now have a machine that looks like the majority of the other bikes racing but don't for one moment think that you simply must do everything. One does see most standard looking machines raced, with only the bare necessities removed in the interests of safety, and doing quite well too. I'm just setting out what you can do if you want to go the whole way.

You may well have noticed machines with brakes fitted that were certainly not fitted when the bike left the factory and also that some of the standard ones had airscoops fitted to aid heat dissipation. Well most manufacturers seem to have listed a racing brake of some sort at least for the bigger models that really do need some more retardation under racing conditions and where an item has been registered then of course its quite legal to use it. Some manufacturers list a disc or even twin discs and in some cases it may be an alternative drum brake like the Fontana 220mm double sided twin leading shoe model fitted to Tridents in particular. Nortons and Hondas fitted with a disc brake list an extra one. But if you are not made of cash then an airscoop fitted to a standard brake can help a bit - and is legal. But don't forget that the extra air has to get out too.

About the last item that you will have noticed before getting around to competing yourself is that of fairings. There are no restrictions here and you can fit any variety that you like, whether it makes provision for a headlamp or not. Now to go on quote directly from the regulations governing machine specifications for the 1972 Production TT Race so that you will have all the regulations governing this branch of the sport.

SPECIFICATION OF A SPORTS PRODUCTION MACHINE FOR ROAD RACES HELD UNDER THE INTERNATIONAL SPORTING CODE OF THE F.I.M. APPLICABLE TO THE 1972 T.T. RACES

1.   Machines must be fully equipped motorcycles built from new components by a motorcycle manufacturer who is recognised as such by the A.C.U. in the case of the United Kingdom or in other cases by the F.M.N. of the country concerned.

2.   The manufacturer or concessionaire (a retail motorcycle dealer cannot act on behalf of a manufacturer or concessionaire) must homologate with the A.C.U. before 29th April, 1972, the full price and specification of the motorcycle, together with details of all optional extras which could be fitted to the machine before it leaves the factory in the first instance. **No part of the General Specification or of any optional extra shall be of such a type as to make it illegal for the machine to be used on any public highway within the United Kingdom.**

3.   The general specification of the motorcycle as homologated by the makers or concessionaires must be strictly adhered to. It must comprise only the type of original or optional components with which, according to the manufacturer's homologated specification, similar models of the same year could have been fitted before leaving the factory.

4.   Not less than 200 machines equipped with the maker's original components and not less than 200 of each item of optional equipment must have been manufactured and sold through the normal trade channels by the closing date of entries, 28th April 1972. An accountant's certificate will be required as proof.

5.   Maker's modifications introduced to machines of the maker's home market may be incorporated in machines which are listed as the same type or model but of earlier or later manufacture, provided that they may be incorporated by the simple process of exchanging one part for another. Brazing, welding or machining to incorporate such modifications is not permitted.

6.   The equipment of every motorcycle must comprise: Electric lighting including generator, kickstart or electrical or other mechanical starting device, exhaust pipe or pipes and efficient silencer or silencers as originally supplied with the machine, and chainguards and primary chaincases which must be adequate to prevent the drive being accidentally touched at any part of the run not in contact with the sprockets.

7.   The motorcycle must comply in every respect with the requirements of the Geneva Convention of 1949, even if the manufacturing country is not a party to that convention.

8.   The engine must function normally on a commercial brand of fuel that is supplied to the public from a wayside pump.

9.   A machine must not vary from the manufacturer's specification as homologated with the A.C.U. in respect of the following characteristics:
   (a)   Frame.
   (b)   Rear suspension system other than damper units.
   (c)   Front forks and suspension.
   (d)   Wheel hubs and brakes (apart from friction linings).
   (e)   Silencers.
   (f)   Diameter of exhaust pipe.
   (g)   Primary chaincases.
   (h)   The electrical equipment all of which must be in working order at the start of the race.

(i)   Carburetters, the quantity, make, type, model, choke size and fitting as listed in the maker's original specification must be used. Air funnel extensions are permitted. A CARBURETTER LISTED AS AN OPTIONAL EXTRA CANNOT BE FITTED OR USED. Fuel injection is not permitted.

(j)   Petrol and oil tanks, the capacity thereof which shall not exceed 24 litres, the material and method of attachment to the machine.

(k)   The type of engine, number of cylinders and stroke.

(l)   The bore may be increased provided the increase does not result in exceeding the limits of the original capacity class for which the machine is recorded by the A.C.U.

(m)   The cylinder and crank cases.

(n)   The materials of which the cylinder head is made.

(o)   The system of operation of induction and exhaust.

(p)   The type of gearbox including the number of speeds.

(q)   The clutch, apart from the friction linings and spring or springs.

(r)   The type of primary and secondary transmission.

10.   The following equipment may be removed — Air cleaners, speedometers.

11.   The following equipment may be varied in the interests of safety or to suit the preference of the driver:

(a)   Exhaust pipes of the same pipe diameter as originally supplied with the machine may have the line of the pipe varied to provide increased ground clearance. However the original pattern of silencer must be retained and the shape must not be altered. The making of "Flats" on silencers will not be permitted. The pipes and silencers must eventually be directed rearwards parallel in plan to the direction of the motion of the vehicles. The gases must not be discharged so as to raise dust or inconvenience a following driver.

(b)   Wheel rims to accomodate racing tyre sizes.

12.   The following alterations to the original specification MUST be carried out in the interests of safety:

(a)   Removal of —
Front and rear registration plates.
Licence holder, club badges other than transfers. Tail light assembly and trafficators,
Centre and prop stands.
Luggage carriers.
Stop lamp switch (or its connection).

(b) High performance or racing tyres must be fitted.

(c) The headlamp glass must be protected by tape or similar material to avoid damage.

13. The addition of the following equipment is permitted.
Flyscreens (wire mesh type recommended).
Security bolts and/or well fillers.
Mudguards and other protective pads.
Airscoops to brakes.
Overflow or breather pipes to existing standard outlets which must be so fitted that they do not enter the exhaust gas stream or do not inconvenience a following driver.
Fairings.

14. Any part not specifically mentioned may be modified to suit the individual preference of the driver provided that in the first instance it was a part which was or could have been supplied as part of the original manufacturer's specification. No temporary parts may be added other than those under permitted modifications. The fitting of any such modified parts must not involve any alteration to any part listed above.

Full details of all modifications must be declared on the entry form, and it will be incumbered upon all drivers or entrants to bring these to the attention of the scrutineers prior to and during the practice periods and again at the pre-race examination.

Fig. 15 — Triumph Daytona. Still the most popular machine in the 500 cc class, at club level anyway. Note the front disc brake — an optional extra permitted for the 1972 season — of Pagehiln manufacture. The bike also has five gears fitted and a 'Thruxton' exhaust system. It finished fourth in the TT and is seen here at Quarter Bridge. Rider Ray Knight. (MCI pic).

Chapter 9
Formula 750

Formula 750 is a natural progression from production racing. Its a small step to simply remove all the parts that are unnecessary if you do not have to have lights, silencers, mudguards etc. So you end up with a stripped roadster on which all possible tuning is permitted short of fitting a supercharger.

As natural as it seems on paper to strip your production racing bike down to the stark minimum, many enter the class by acquiring a suitable roadster engine and installing it in a racing chassis and then giving it the tuning works. And indeed its a comparitively cheap way of getting an instant racer but its not quite as easy as it sounds on paper.

Like production racing the class was seen initially as providing a racing class that did not require a fortune in which to participate successfully. It was hoped that factory support for the class would be forthcoming and that the variety of machines on the grid would provide a much needed stimulus for racing which at an International level has been in the doldrums for many a year with single make domination in the bigger capacity classes.

There are many similarities with production racing though. The same system of homologation of alternative items to the specification is employed. Take first your standard roadster as the basis and then lets see what may be done to make it more competitive within the regulations.

The first major item is that it is permissable to change the frame. But not just any old frame. In fact only frames that the original manufacturer approves of and has, once again - homologated, may be used. As an example both Norton and Triumph approve well known frame manufacturers like Colin Seeley and Rickmans. In any case both companies have registered their own manufactured alternative frames for Formula 750 class racing.

Brakes also come in for many changes but then forks are also changed as well to accommodate various wheels and brakes.

While you have almost limitless possibilities when it comes to tuning up the motor there are nevertheless restrictions so that the original concept is not lost and people with unlimited money start making their own special cylinderheads etc. In fact the cylinderhead and barrel castings must remain the same and likewise the gearbox casting. Alternative gears would, like the production class, be listed as an extra.

One of the principal things that you can do to the motor that you can't do in the production class is to have a free hand with regard to carburetters. This really makes a difference on a racing engine and conversely by sticking to the standard one on a production bike it certainly restricts the tuning possibilities.

Since specifications are so very much looser in the Formula class there is little to dwell upon so its worth a little reflection on the newest class in racing. Several factors have combined to produce it but probably the chief stimulus was provided by the Triumph Trident and Honda four coming onto the market.

This and the evergreen and updated Norton Commando soon collectively acquired the group title of Superbikes and then a 750 class began to feature regularly in National programmes where previously there had only been the odd 1,000cc race to provide variety in the programmes.

Motorcycle News then sponsored a Superbike series and then came the ACU National Championship. In 1971 there was a class included for them within the 500 Mile production race at Thruxton and then a proper race in the TT programme. Meanwhile in the States the formula that restricted machines other than side valves (and only Harley Davidson produced a racing side valve engine) to a capacity limit of 500ccs while the HD could use 750cc at the prestigeous Daytona meeting, was relaxed to 750 for all and they came up with a class from 251cc to 750 but based upon production engines.

This AMA (equivelant of our own ACU) class was adopted over here and indeed has now been accepted in principal by the FIM with the strong possibility of there being a European Championship for the class in 1973 and a world Championship in '74.

But to return to the possible machine for this class that you may want to build from scratch, or out of your production bike, the machine requirements as set out for the 1972 TT 750 Formula TT follow:

SPECIFICATION OF A "FORMULA 750" MOTORCYCLE FOR ROAD RACES HELD UNDER THE INTERNATIONAL SPORTING CODE OF THE F.I.M.

1.   The motorcycle must have originated as a motorcycle built from new components by a motorcycle manufacturer which has been manufactured or

offered for sale as a standard catalogued model to the general public within the territory of an F.M.N.

2. The manufacturer or concessionaire (a retail motorcycle dealer cannot act on behalf of a manufacturer or concessionaire) must homologate with its F.M.N. by 31st October each year the specification of the motorcycle, together with details of all optional components. Only applications received by that date and for motorcycles manufactured during the preceding five years will be considered for use during the following year. After 31st October and before 1st January, the F.M.N. will publish lists of those motorcycles which have been homologated for the following year. No motorcycle can be homologated until all the requirements of the formula have been complied with.
(Note: For 1972 the homologation date is amended to 29th April).

3. Not less than 200 machines equipped with the maker's or listed optional components must have been manufactured or offered for sale as a standard catalogued model to the general public within the territory of the F.M.N. through the normal trade channels.

4. There shall be only one type and size of engine which exceeds 250cc. but does not exceed 750cc. and one of transmission unit for each model homologated.

5. Not less than 200 machines equipped with the maker's original or listed optional components must have been manufactured or offered for sale through the normal trade channels. Documentary evidence of this and that the models have been seen will be required.

6. A machine must not vary from the manufacturer's homologated specification in respect of the following characteristics:
   (a) Type of engine, number of cylinders and stroke.
   (b) Cylinder bore subject to a permitted maximum oversize of 1 mm and subject also to a maximum capacity of 750cc.
   (c) (i) Cylinder barrel in the case of 4 stroke machines.
       (ii) Cylinder barrel material and number of ports in the case of 2 stroke models.
   (d) Crankcase casting.
   (e) Cylinder head casting.
   (f) Gearbox case casting.
   (g) The system of operation of induction and exhaust.
   (h) The type of transmission, i.e. the method of primary driver and number of speeds.

7.   The following characteristics of the motorcycle can only be varied by the substitution of components approved for use by the manufacturer of the original motorcycle concerned after the notification of such approval has been accepted by the F.M.N.:

(a)   Frame.
(b)   Front forks.
(c)   Wheels including hubs and brakes.
(d)   Wheel spindles.

8.   The petrol tanks of any motorcycle shall have a 6 litres minimum and a 24 litres maximum capacity.

9.   True fuel injection where the fuel is injected directly into the combustion chamber of the engine is not permitted.

10.   In all other respects the motorcycle must conform with the International Sporting Code of the F.I.M.

Fig. 16 – A formula 750 Moto Guzzi racing version of the roadster. This one finished third in the 1971 24 Hour Bol d'Or race, held on the short Le Mans circuit. Rider Vittorio Brambilla. (MCI pic).

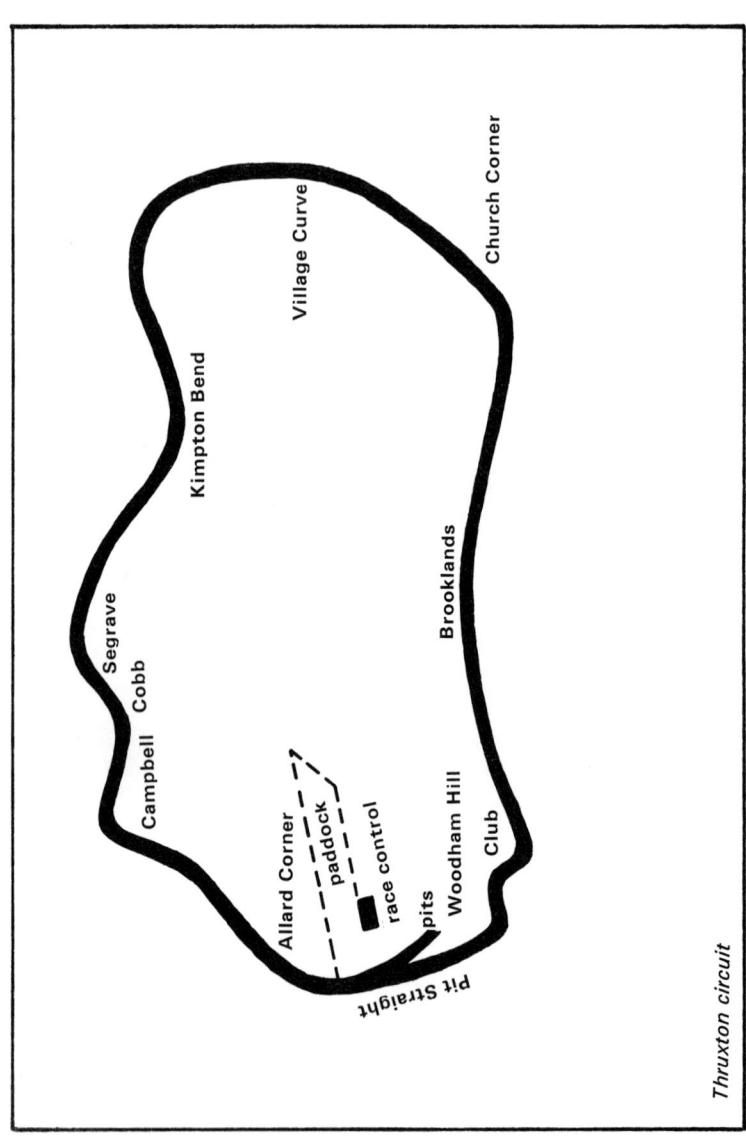

Thruxton circuit

Church Corner

Village Curve

Kimpton Bend

Segrave

Campbell Cobb

Allard Corner

paddock

race control

pits

Woodham Hill

Club

Brooklands

Pit Straight

Chapter 10
The circuits

Thruxton is the present home of the Motor Cycle 500 Mile Grand Prix, to give the race its full name, and this circuit possesses features which are seldom found anywhere else except for the Isle of Man. If Brands Hatch is the mecca of the short circuit scratcher then Thruxton suits those who prefer very fast, in places flat out, curves and the wide open spaces.

It is fairly easy to get a quick bike round reasonably fast. But to really get the times down you have to be able to place the machine precisely without the advantages of obvious landmarks and have enough nerve to lay the bike right over with it all wound on in top gear, and to negotiate bumps while so doing. As you can imagine under those conditions the bike will leave the ground completely and it takes some getting used to.

To tell you that the last 500 Miler (1969) was won at an average speed of over 84 mph should convey that the track is really high speed stuff and in fact the lap record for bikes is 91 mph, so there is a lot of time spent at over 100 mph. The start and finish are situated just before a particularly fast and testing right hand bend called Allard Corner, and while this is full bore on even a 750cc class machine accelerating off the line, approached after a run past the pits it is one where you can make up much time, or lose it if you don't grit your teeth and hang on. There is a rather convenient peeling-off point here to set you up nicely for this one and it is the marker board indicating 100 yds. Sticking right on the outside of the track until the board and then pulling the bike over hard and aiming for the apex will get you round nicely. There are however one or two bumps that are best avoided if you can spot them.

If you are riding a bike with plenty of poke and four gears you may well find yourself caught between using third or fourth gear for this one. A 500 can just take it flat in top but the motor will not yet have achieved full speed from the previous bend. A 250 really makes time on the big machines here as they can go round without slowing at all. Allard is a good test of navigation as the bumpy bits really make a fast machine move about. It's easy to peel off too early for this one which gets you in trouble on the way out and you'll have to knock it off to get back on course. Taking Allard fast takes you to the outside of the track on the slightly uphill left hand section approaching Campbell bend. It's just here while breasting the rise that you get carried to the inside of the track and in the wrong place for the approaching sharp right hander, and to make matters worse there is a slight down gradient on the run-in which makes braking a little more difficult. The correct line through Campbell can give a faster time through the succeeding two corners of Cobb and Segrave. This is a good instance of where the fastest line through the first corner would result in being slower through the section as a whole.

Taking Campbell so that you end up right on the inside of the circuit can set you up so that Cobb and Segrave can be taken on full acceleration, giving a faster entry into the very fast Kimpton Bend section, which is a real nerve tester.

Kimpton can be taken flat-out by everything but the very fastest bikes. This section has a succession of ripples on the way through, most of which can be avoided by peeling off late and keeping the bike as tight as possible to the outside. The key to the bend is in the peeling off point. There are no marks to guide the eye and I run alongside the grass on the inside of the circuit until forced to make the long left sweep, laying the bike over as hard as possible to miss the rippled on the way out.

Getting this one right makes the difference to Goodwood, which is the next of Thruxton's high speed curves. The right exit from Kimpton will set you up for Goodwood, The entry for this one is really the wide open spaces with nothing to guide you. About the only clues I can give here are to aim yourself at the marshal's post before peeling off. Village curve is where the track seems awfully narrow as on full-chat and laid hard over you have to try not to roll it off. The secret is not to as this will lead to the bike finding its way towards the outside of the circuit and trouble. The long continuing curve, like no other that I have come across, has only one feature before starting the climb up the hill past the big aircraft hangar and this stretch is called Brooklands.

The feature I mentioned is at Church Corner where right on the apex of the curve, rather than corner, there is a hump in the surface where even a quick 250 can completely leave the ground, the 750s are real fun. The secret is yet once again to leave it late before laying the bike over so as to straight-line the apex and take the jump in a straight line. Taken round the outside of the hump you run on to some ripples that send you curtsying towards the outside and the grass verge; taking it in a curve produces some interesting results when you land from the resulting bounds achieved by the machine. The only real way is keep it all wound on, set yourself and hang on over the jump - taken in a straight line and landing in one, all is well.

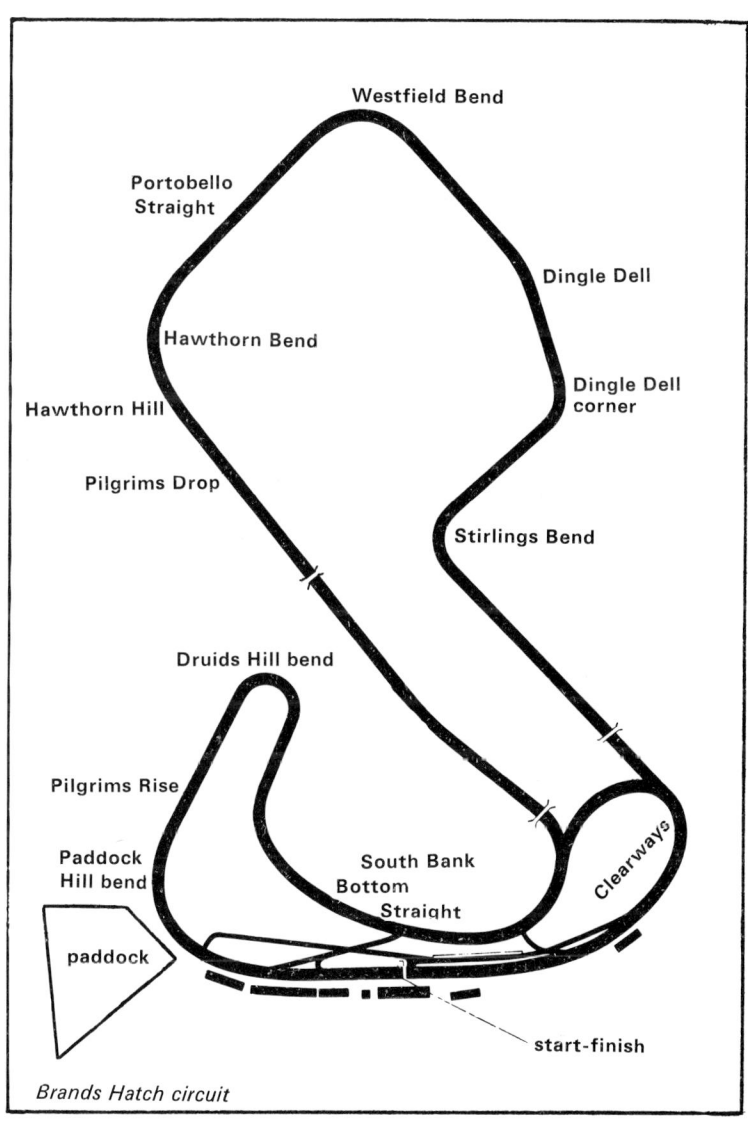

Westfield Bend

Portobello
Straight

Dingle Dell

Hawthorn Bend

Dingle Dell
corner

Hawthorn Hill

Pilgrims Drop

Stirlings Bend

Druids Hill bend

Pilgrims Rise

Paddock
Hill bend

South Bank
Bottom
Straight

Clearways

paddock

start-finish

Brands Hatch circuit

Up the hill and the last item on the agenda at Thruxton is Club Corner. This is difficult because the approach is a gentle curve while you are actually braking hard, which can be interesting. There seem to be two ways to tackle this one and I'm not sure which is the best. Using the brakes to the absolute maximum you can start from the outside of the circuit and brake as far as is possible in a straight line across the track to finish up right on the inside of the right hand section of the very tight, almost chicane, 'S' bend. The other way gives a better run-in to the first part of the corner but to do this means keeping more to the outside and blending your curved entry into the first part of the section. This is probably better from the purist point of view but if you were dicing closely it could let another man take the advantage by getting on the inside of the first part. Then you would probably have to give way because there is only room for one line through the double curved corner. And then for the run up to the chequered flag.

Brands Hatch

Brands Hatch is really three circuits in one. The short Club circuit is 1.24 mile long and is used for, appropriately enough, club events mainly. There is the full Grand Prix course of 2.65 miles long and then for the Hutchinson 100 races the events are run in the reverse direction, and this makes it an altogether different challenge indeed.

The names Paddock Bend and Brands are synonymous. This bend has caught out the best - even World Champion Giacomo Agostini. There are few others that even resemble it. The approach is uphill from the pit area out in top gear, and the thing that upsets the normal approach is that you can't make a quick estimation where to brake because suddenly the brow of the hill is behind you and the track disappears round the corner and downhill out of sight. Practice and a memory for every bump are the only real solutions. As a guide though, use the 100 yard marker board, not to brake by, but to set yourself in the right spot for the long curve round and down. There are a succession of ripples just on the braking line which can easily upset you and develop into more than just a shimmy if you are just laying it over at the time you hit them. Try and straight-line the run-in while doing the heavy braking and a marker to aim for just before peeling off is the marshal's point where the access road joins the track by the competitors' stand. Getting the power on early here helps to steady the bike and the apex for which you aim is rather deceptively further round the corner that it seems at first sight.

Druids Bend is a real hairpin and this type of acute bend is one where all the rules on cornering and the approach to them are broken because it almost seems that any line is as fast as any other in the general hurly burly of short circuit competition. Take the outside line and somebody will try to get inside and the other way round and they will try the outside. For a personal preference I take the inside line. Trying to get round the outside means being 'taken up the road' if the man on the outside slides off and anyway it must be a little farther round the outside.

There is little to be said about the next feature - Bottom Bend. It's a straight forward left hander taken from the outside—inside, but with one reservation, there always seems to be a slight damp patch on a dull day about a foot out from edge that can lead to an unexpected slither. Bottom Straight is a bit of a misnomer in that if one is travelling fairly rapidly it's not straight at all but one long curve, and before you know where you are it's time to peel off for what is Kidney Bend on the short circuit and South Bank on the long one. This is a fairly straightforward left-right flick from one side to the other but the exit from the last part sets you up for Clearways where, like Paddock Bend, much time can be lost, particularly when there is a tight bunch scrapping for a place.

The best entry to Clearways is made from almost on the grass which is rather convenient because this permits straight-lining the exit from Kidney and therefore the heavy braking necessary can be done in a straight-line. Like Paddock this one also drops away and you have to know where you are going without being able to see at a glance. And so back to the start/finish. Along this straight a big twin could be approaching 110mph and so the gearing should be that which about matches this speed to the revs you want to achieve in top gear. On a 650 Triumph for instance this might be a 19T gearbox sprocket and a 46T rear wheel sprocket giving approx 4.8 overall ratio. Achieving 7,000 rpm in top would then give a theoretical 112mph but beware of taking paper calculations as gospel because different sizes of tyres and wheels alter things somewhat. The figures given were for 19in wheels, for 18 they would be reduced by about 3mph. An even more significant point to remember in this connection is that you can often kid yourself that you are going faster than you are by taking rev counter readings too literally. When the circuit is a bit on the bumpy side you can get a significant amount of wheelspin - or wheel hop - which gives a false reading for the purposes of calculating mph. The speed is of no importance of itself, it's the revs that you achieve that matters, and on what gearing.

For club racing purposes you will probably only be concerned with the short circuit but it's possible that there will again be National status events on the Grand Prix circuit, and there could well be a production race on the programme so a few notes might be useful. After Bottom Straight on the short circuit, instead of entering Kidney Bend the long version goes on and on in a tight

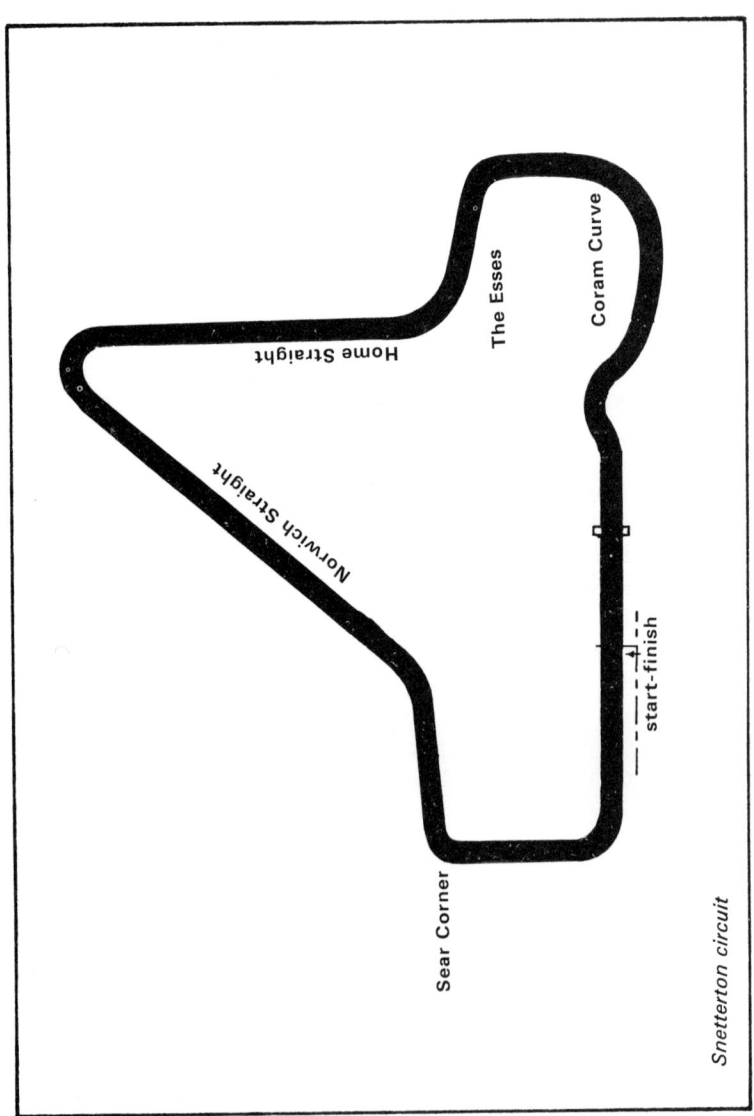

Snetterton circuit

lefthander that is a real tester, and then on to the fastest part of the track, the downhill Pilgrims Drop. Here you would need a higher gear, either a rear cog with two teeth less or a gearbox with one tooth more. The succeeding Hawthorn Bend is a straightforward right hander except that it's bumpy on the way out, a comment that also applies to the one after the Portobello Straight.

Dingle Dell Corner is awkward because the approach is deceptively fast after the swoop through the dip at Dingle Dell and the 100yd marker board is a very useful landmark here. Stirling's Bend next, ordinary left hander and then rejoin the short circuit at Clearways, but this time the approach is of course much faster and the track camber almost adverse.

The circuit in reverse is only used for the Hutchinson 100 which is of International status and by the time you get to that stage you will have formed your own ideas on lines through a corner. Suffice to say that the speeds achieved are similar, as are the lap times and gearing.

Snetterton

The main feature of Snetterton is the 1,000 yd long Norwich Straight which will allow all but the very fastest machines to reach their true maximum speed.

Snetterton has features guaranteed to test most aspects of a machine's performance, particularly braking and roadholding.

It starts with a slightly uphill run to Riches, at first sight a normal right hander. However, it is almost a double apex corner and the ripples in the surface will set any machine weaving about a little. Peeling off at a point actually just outside the dotted white line denoting the outside of the track and clipping the grass where it juts out into the track sets you nicely for the exit - on the way out almost clipping, again, the grass just by the marshal's post, and yet again, getting inside the dotted white line at the track's edge. However, if it is wet, just here on the exit from the corner it gets rather slippery and should be taken wider.

Sears Corner follows, no secrets here, and then into the left hander running in to the Norwich Straight. Naturally, the faster you can get through these two and the faster your entry into the Straight the faster you'll be going before you shut-off at the end, because even though the Straight is that long over 500cc bikes can still be accelerating. On this left hander without a name there are a succession of ripples that can cause you to drift on the grass in the centre of the track if you do not make sure to keep as far as possible to the left.

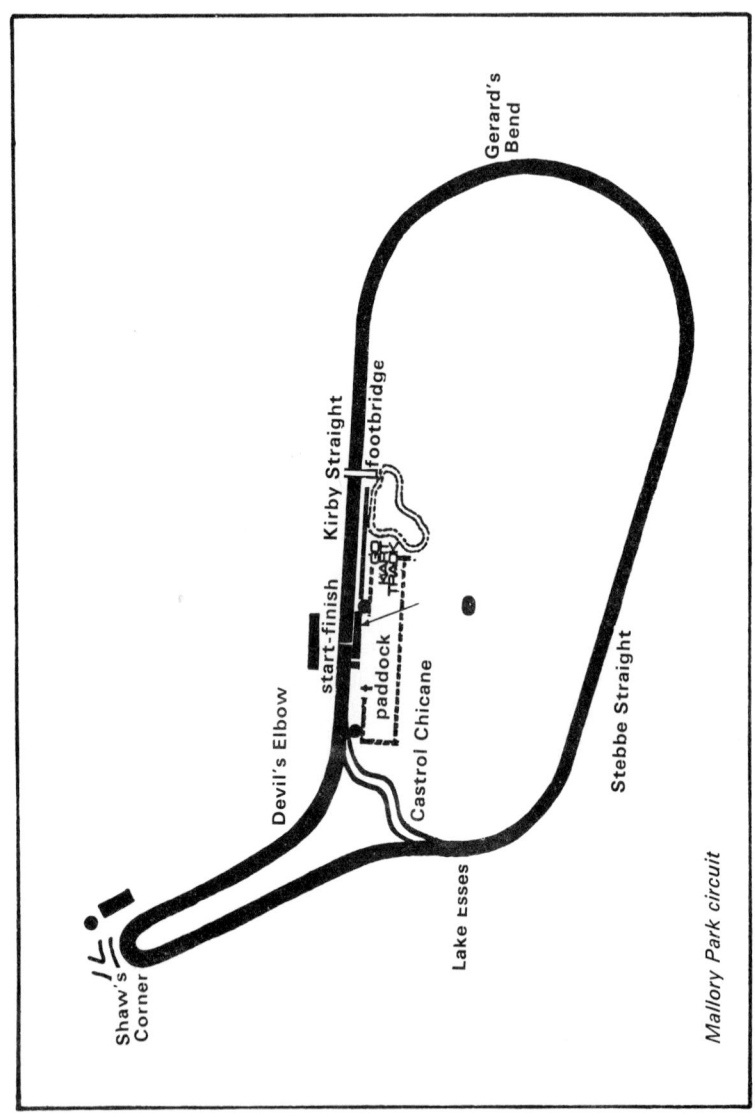

Shaw's Corner

Devil's Elbow

start-finish

Kirby Straight

footbridge

Gerard's Bend

paddock

Castrol Chicane

Lake Esses

Stebbe Straight

Mallory Park circuit

86

At the end of the straight one has one of the greatest tests of brakes on short circuit racing, when you reduce speed from near maximum possible to take the Hairpin at maybe 40mph. At this point the technique of picking a particular braking point can really pay off over the 'guess it every time method'. After a rush down the Home Straight the Esses are next, a sharp left right. This is an occasion where trying to get through the first part too fast can put you in the wrong place to take the second part to the best advantage and you can end up slower than another man, though entering the section faster. It pays to be just a shade slower on the first part so as to be able to get over to the left hand side - to be able to drive through harder.

Coram Curve follows almost immediately, a long continuing bend taken flat out on a 250, maybe just on a quick 500, and rolling it off a shade on a 650. Smaller machines can get some advantage here as when the bigger bikes have to ease-up a little they can pull back a few feet. Bigger machines tend to find the hump on the way in to the corner a little unsettling but it's a mistake to ease the throttle there because this is far more likely to provoke a wobble than if you keep it wound on and grit your teeth. The entry point to Coram is rather later than you might think from just riding round quick, rather than going as hard as possible. Also it can pay to change in to a higher ratio before entering the bend rather than having to change halfway round.

'Russells' is the last feature to complete the circuit and this is a really fast left-right taken as fast as your nerves will let you. There is little to tell except that the little extra bit of track outside the dotted white line on the way in can be useful to set you up right for the last part - and the run up to the finish.

Mallory Park

Mallory Park is similar to Brands Hatch in several ways, offering in its 1.35 miles real challenges to nerve, brakes and roadholding. It is a tight circuit with lap times under the minute close dicing and requiring gearing similar to Brands.

From the start/finish there is plenty of time for you to get sorted out on the approach to the first corner, a notorious bend called Gerards. This is so because it just goes on seemingly forever, and takes you right through 180°. Going in to this one there are a series of bumps guaranteed to set most machines moving about a bit. Due to the length of this bend it seems to make little difference where you peel off but everyone seems to rush into it at what seems on first impressions a fair rate of knots. It's a bend where as you go further round you can increase your throttle opening and it's then a struggle to keep the bike from

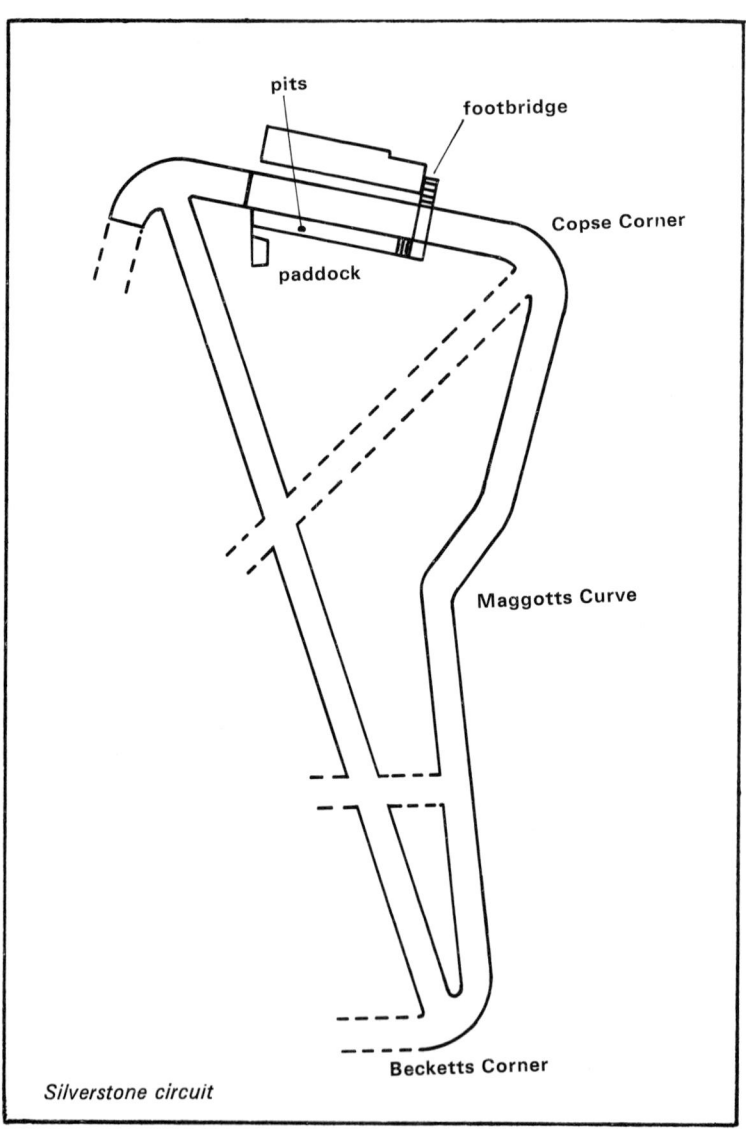

pits

footbridge

Copse Corner

paddock

Maggotts Curve

Becketts Corner

Silverstone circuit

running wide. Again this is a bend where the speed through largely determines the maximum down the following straight. This is called Stebbe Straight and it leads into the Esses past the lake. It takes nerve to get through really quickly and this is where you will see the quick men making time most noticeably on the slower ones. There is a braking marker for guidance on the way in, a quick flick right left and there is just time to get the throttle wide open for a few yards before crash braking for Shaw's Corner.

Shaw's is so slow that it hardly seems true. First gear and another hairpin where the line seems to matter not too much, though my own preference is to keep as tight as possible as I feel that it allows you to get the power on a little earlier, and in any case positions you on the inside of the track where you want to be to take the Devil's Elbow.

Rather like Paddock Hill in reverse, you can't see where this one is going as you approach it. It disappears over the hill and drops away to the left and as you go round, the solid looking barrier confronting you on the inside of the track is a deterrent to winding it on flat-out although this is possible even on a very quick production bike. Apart from all this the bend is a bumpy one to boot, just to make life a little more interesting - and then the run to the finishing flag.

Silverstone

Silverstone might well be described as the ideal beginners' course. It's where I had my first speed event in 1958. There are few things to hit around the outside. Plenty of room if you run out of road and all the four corners are straight forward, on top of that it's flat too. There are two circuits but the Grand Prix circuit is not for motorcycles these days. The club short circuit is 1.608 miles long and is fast enough to really let a big machine go so that gearing would be high for a big twin, say aim for a 120mph.

From the wide open spaces on the grid you rush up to the first bend and it's Copse Corner. There are braking markers to aid the approach and the conventional line is the one that pays here. Right from the outside near the grass, engage third if you have a four speed box and accelerate round getting the bike very close to the small wall on the inside near the apex. As you come out the track seems to open out so wide that it looks like an airfield and of course Silverstone is one of the tracks that have been airfields in their time.

Having navigated the smooth corner there is plenty of time to aim the bike at the right hand side of the track to line up to take Maggots curve which is flat-out

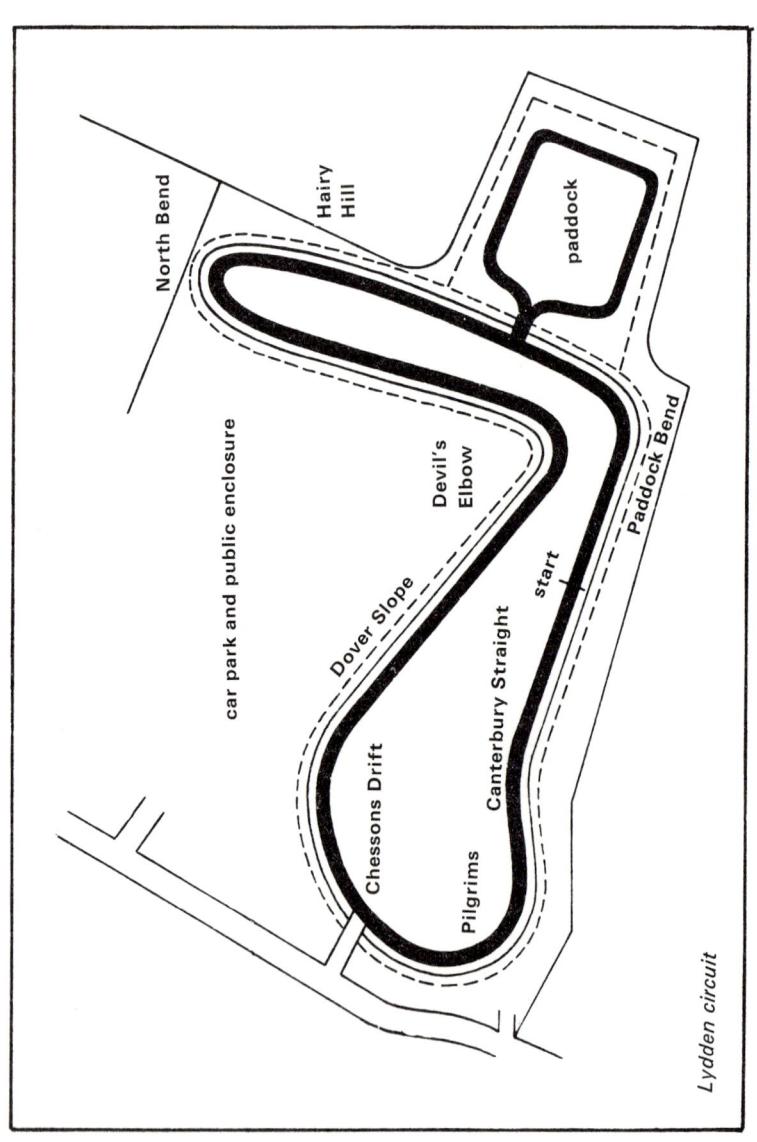

North Bend

Hairy Hill

paddock

car park and public enclosure

Devil's Elbow

Dover Slope

Paddock Bend

Canterbury Straight

start

Chessons Drift

Pilgrims

Lydden circuit

even on a big bike. On a good day it can be taken at an indicated 110mph on the speedo and while going in flat-out presents no problems it's the ripples on the exit that may cause you trouble. Be ready for the model to shake its head but keep the throttle open and the bike on the same line. Rolling it off and trying to straighten up can get you into trouble.

Having probably put the wind up yourself by cornering at that sort of speed - maximum - you then find yourself rushing full bore at Becketts, which on the club circuit is an acute hairpin. To aid your braking not only are there a couple of marker boards but also painted lines across the track so there is no real excuse for being in trouble with your braking and having said that I remember running out of the road there myself.

Round Becketts and the straight wide track disappears over just a slight rise into the horizon. In fact the straight is about three quarters of a mile long, long enough for the fastest bikes to get there first however fast you come out of the hairpin. But from maximum you have to get down to something like 50mph to take Woodcote corner, and it's bumpy and precedes the run up to the flag, so somebody is always trying to rush up the inside of you. Again the conventional line - outside, apex, outside, is the best one and the only problems are presented by the bumps as you exit.

Lydden

The one mile long track frequently offers some of the closest dicing to be found on any short circuit. It is so short and tortuous that it is possible for a smaller bike to equal, or even beat, a big machine since there is no chance at all to use superior speed. In fact much emphasis is placed upon braking capabilities and a lighter machine with good brakes can easily outbrake a heavier one, thus off-setting the bigger bike's better acceleration. To make the point I've actually had a 500 in front at the flag there with a 250 close behind.

Gearing for Lydden is just as low as it is possible to get, and then you will probably only use the first three gears anyway. I doubt if you exceed 90mph at the fastest points. Certainly from the start there is just time to get buzzing hard in second gear and you have to get set for the first corner, This is approached through a slight kink left and a decline before taking the long right that takes you right back on yourself. Exaggerating the left hander gives a desirable late peeling off point for the right, and this is doubly difficult, one because it is a tightening corner and two because it has an awkward bump on the apex that causes the front wheel to leave the ground momentarily, particularly as the track

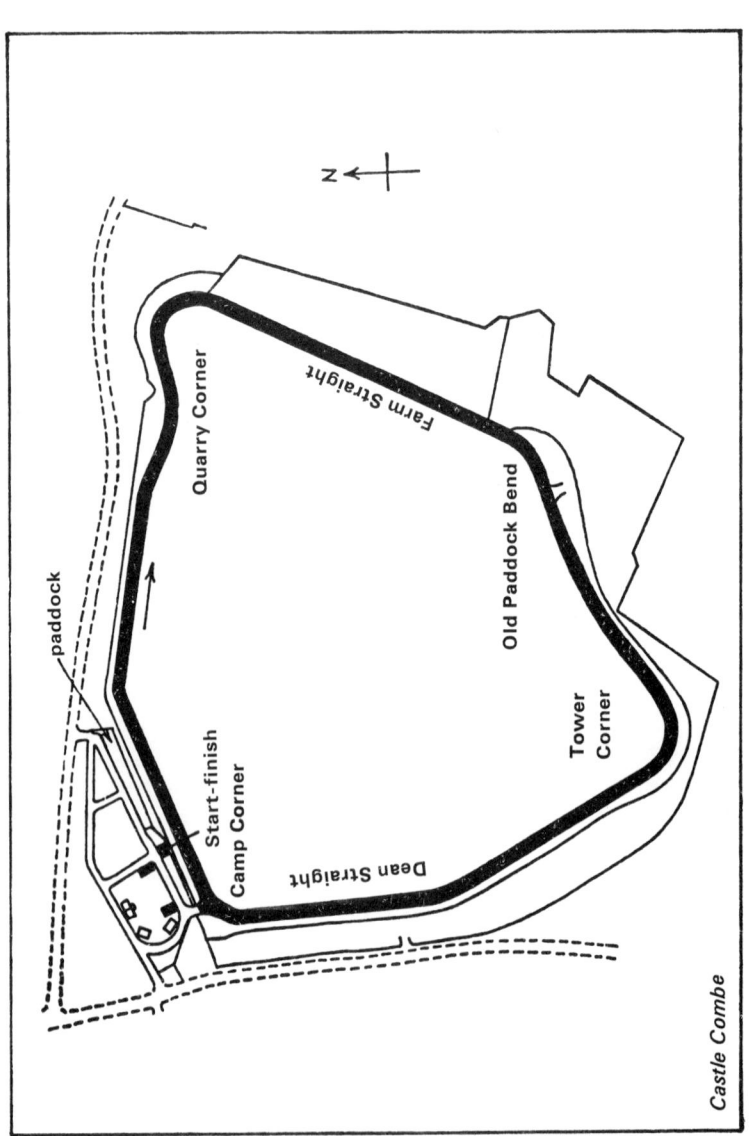

Castle Combe

curves up the side of a hill, and can catch you unawares and throw the bike off line. One or two ripples in the surface further aggravate the situation and unless the bike is kept tight in to the inside there is a danger of running off line while accelerating round Chesson's Drift.

The run down to the only real left hander on the track makes the braking difficult to estimate but the Marshal's post on the inside of the circuit gives some guide. It's a bumpy, sharp left hander with a camber slightly against you and a quick passage through this one can make for considerable advantage in the climb up Hairy Hill. The Hairpin that follows is a real tight one and It's the tight line that pays here. The Hairpin is so tight that speed is necessarily very slow and the temptation is to bang the throttle open as you come out, but there is usually, a fair amount of rubber about here and it's too easy for the rear wheel to break away.

Paddock Bend is the last one to tackle and at first sight this is a straightforward right hander but the fact that many have bitten the dust here indicates that it is indeed a little more difficult than it seems. It's easy to lay the bike over a little too early, consequently you get carried out towards the edge on the way out and you find yourself in trouble. Ripples on the way in can be awkward too and set the machine weaving enough to upset your line, and you join the spectators. The approach is difficult because you rush sharply downhill, and this tends to make you peel off early, because you can see the bank rushing at you. In fact the best line requires the nerve to leave the peel-off point quite late then lay it over hard, and on this one there is no alternative to going in on the overrun. One word of caution, if you do run wide on the exit the track drops away at the edge.

Castle Combe

The Combe is a forgiving circuit. It's not difficult to get round reasonably quickly but due to the obvious lack of landmarks that little extra requires a lot of concentration and application. Still, there is plenty of grass around and from the start there is a flat-out right hander to be taken before the very interesting Quarry Corner. The Corner itself is nothing more than a sharp right but the approach is via a right/left kink that upsets the line into it nicely, plus a series of ripples, unless you get right in to the track on the outside, then this also sets you up for the long right leading into Farm Straight.

Old Paddock Bend requires a fair degree of nerve, as does any corner that is taken nearly as fast as the bike will go. It requires just a touch of the brakes or

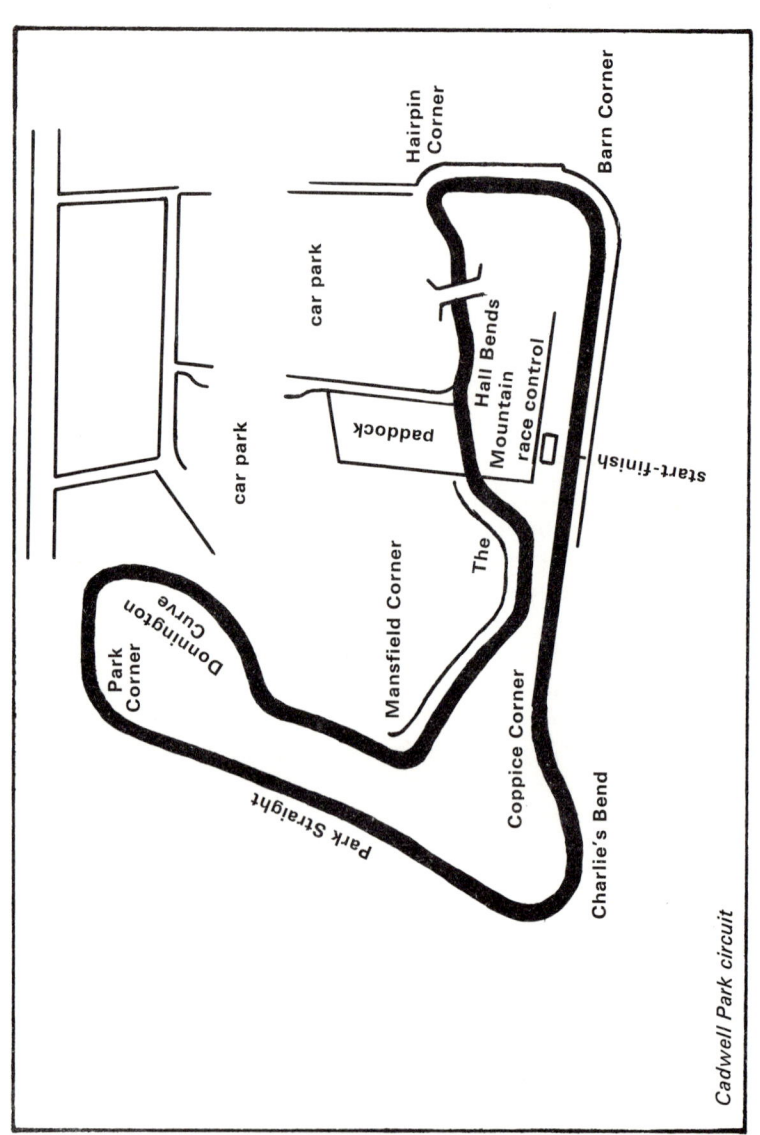

Cadwell Park circuit

Hairpin Corner

Barn Corner

car park

car park

Hall Bends

paddock

Mountain

race control

start-finish

car park

Mansfield Corner

The

Coppice Corner

Donnington Curve

Park Corner

Park Straight

Charlie's Bend

94

engaging a lower gear. Tower Corner is typical of the other corners at Castle Combe, you can see round them, they are wide and lack features from which to place yourself, and the 'mechanical' approach does not work quite so well here. Once round Old Paddock you tuck away again for the run up to Tower Corner, another sharp right with few distinguishing marks and one about which you always feel that you should have taken it faster.

After this, the slightly uphill run towards the curve in Dean Straight, which requires no easing off and then an equally slight decline to Camp Corner, which is where you joined the circuit when you went out to the grid. There is nothing difficult about this one, again it's very wide and it's not until you get the speed just right that you find yourself carried out on the right line. There are, however, ripples on the corner but not until you are trying really hard will they prove awkward. The fastest speed will probably be reached on the Camp-Quarry section but only on a particularly quick production bike will you approach 120mph.

Cadwell Park

Cadwell is at once three circuits, scenic, tortuous and testing. There are; the Club Circuit, the Woodlands Circuit and the full 2¼ mile Grand Prix Circuit. Club racing is generally held on the more hilly section away from the main Paddock. Even this can be either 1.3 or 1.5 miles long depending on which of the two Hairpin Bends is used to bisect the GP track. Using the Club version, the start/finish is situated after Mansfield Corner and there is just enough of the downhill run to whichever Hairpin is being used to sort things out before braking, and the brakes get a real testing. The inside line round the Hairpin is the one this time because the camber is against you on the way out and you won't get the best run at the very steep hill which leads up to Charlie's Bend.

Charlie's is a tester for the nerves and the 'lay it over till everything touches' brigade will probably get round first as, again, the camber is not favourable and the grass gets awfully close. Also the corner goes up over a hill so you can't see round it and your judgement must be right and based on experience, it's not one with which to take liberties. Rounding Charlie's you then go hard downhill for a while down Park Straight and up the other side where you rush up over the crest and arrive at Park Corner in a great hurry. However, there is a convenient braking marker board and it's right down the box to second on nearly all models for the sharp right, and there is a short straight before tackling Donnington Curve. This is a problem on a big machine as you are accelerating hard while laid over all the way round and then the curve tightens up and you start

Fig. 17 — A formula 750 Suzuki being refuelled during the American Daytona 200 mile race. Aircraft type quick fillers are used and the hose can be seen in the side of the tank, the system is self-sealing. Rider Ron Grant. (MCI pic).

to go downhill and flick the model on to opposite bank to take the Gooseneck left hander. Then follows a steep downhill section approaching Mansfield and this is a particularly difficult one for braking as there are no real pointers, and if you miscalculate, and it's so easy, you take up grass-tracking instead of road-racing, fortunately there is plenty available.

After you have thought that you were going to run out of road at Mansfield, at least if you have taken it fast enough you will, then it's the gentle downhill run back to the Hairpin and past the start/finish.

Well I've not ridden on every track in the British Isles, perhaps not too surprisingly as there are quite a few round the country. Some are used just a few times in a season and particular clubs have obtained from the owners, permission to run their own meetings which means joining those clubs if you want to ride there, and what with being in about six clubs already anyway there just is not sufficient racing days in a season to get round to them all. Likewise there are meetings just about every weekend and one naturally tends to travel the shorter distances to tracks that one prefers.

The first of those clubs that have managed to survive without my membership is the Darley Moor Club and they are in the unique position of owning their own circuit. The 1½ mile long track is a tight one with speeds in the 60-70s mph. They do feature production races in the programme. The other three tracks for which we can only offer a track diagram are all Northern ones; Silloth, Croft and Llandow.

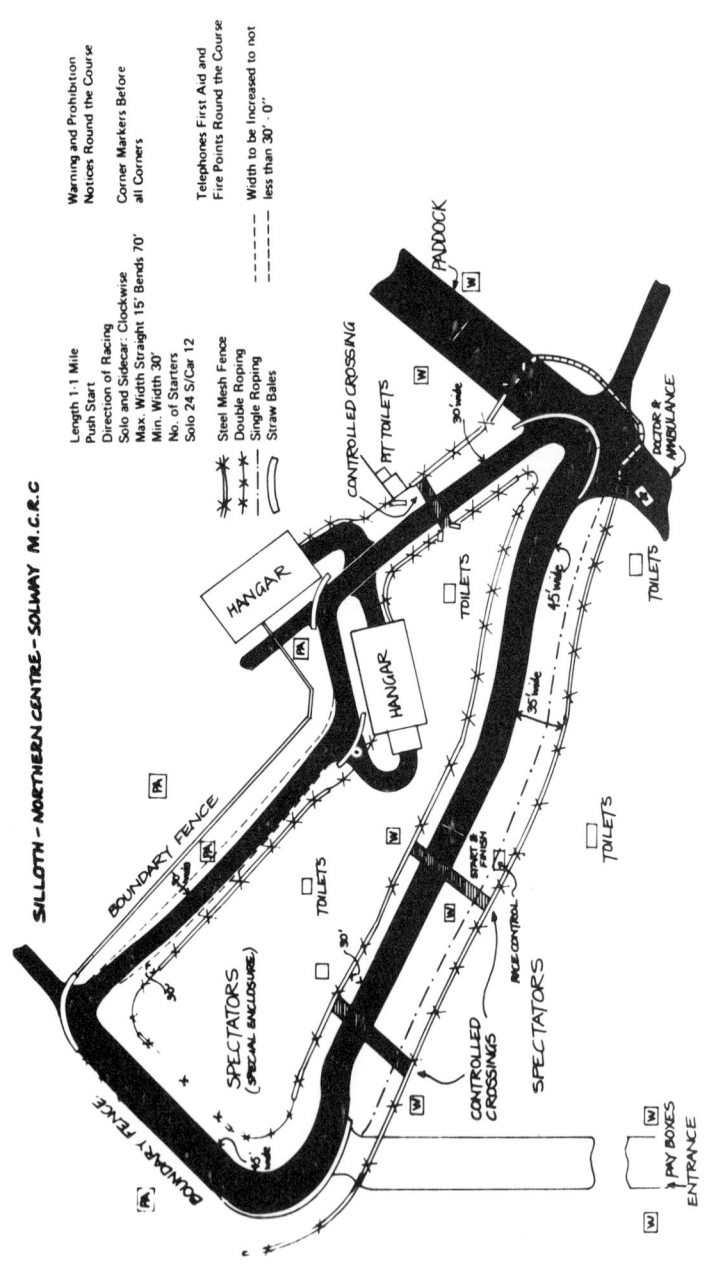

SILLOTH – NORTHERN CENTRE – SOLWAY M.C.R.C.

Length 1·1 Mile
Push Start
Direction of Racing
Solo and Sidecar: Clockwise
Max. Width Straight 15' Bends 70'
Min. Width 30'
No. of Starters
Solo 24 S/Car 12

Steel Mesh Fence
Double Roping
Single Roping
Straw Bales

Warning and Prohibition
Notices Round the Course

Corner Markers Before
all Corners

Telephones First Aid and
Fire Points Round the Course

Width to be Increased to not
less than 30' · 0"

PADDOCK

CONTROLLED CROSSING

PIT TOILETS

DOCTOR &
AMBULANCE

30' wide

TOILETS

45' wide

TOILETS

HANGAR

HANGAR

BOUNDARY FENCE

35' wide

TOILETS

START &
FINISH

RACE CONTROL

TOILETS

30'

30'

SPECTATORS
(SPECIAL ENCLOSURE)

BOUNDARY FENCE

CONTROLLED
CROSSING

SPECTATORS

PAY BOXES
ENTRANCE

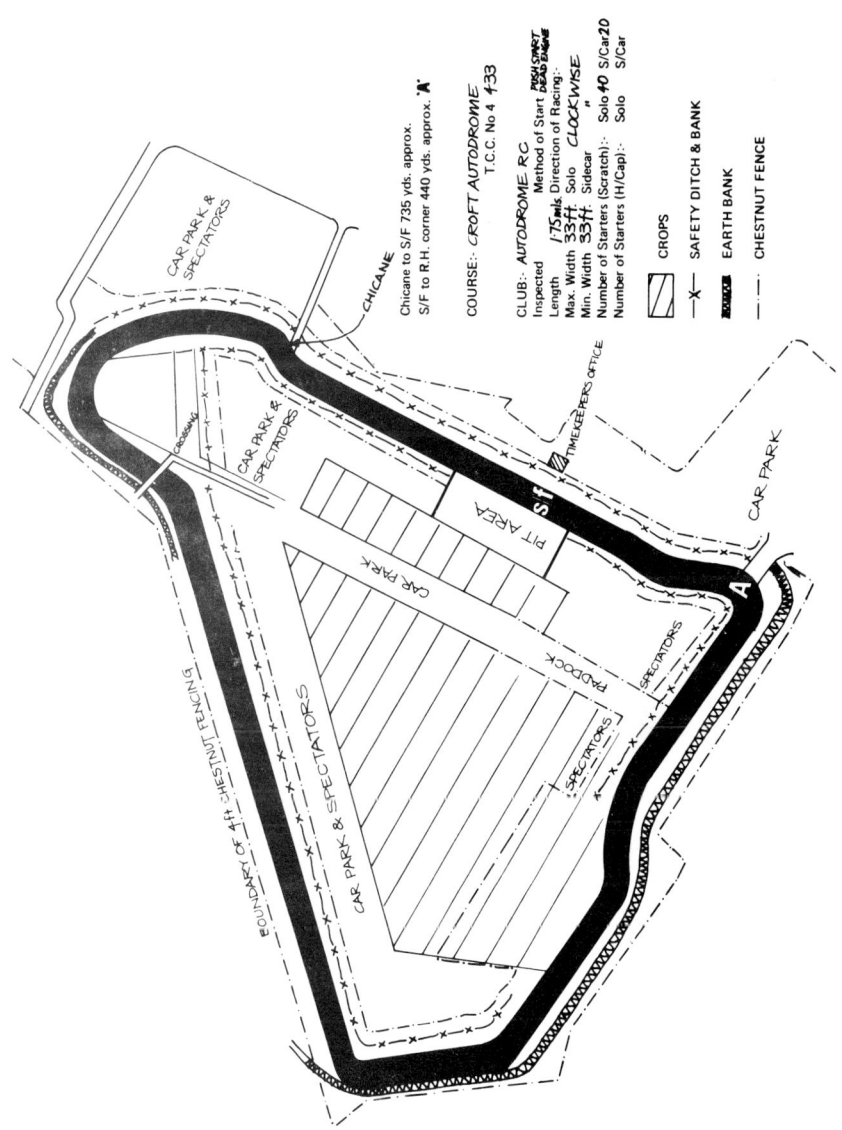

CAR PARK & SPECTATORS

CHICANE

Chicane to S/F 735 yds. approx.
S/F to R.H. corner 440 yds. approx. 'X'

COURSE:: *CROFT AUTODROME*
T.C.C. No 4 †33

CLUB:: *AUTODROME R.C.*
Inspected
Length   *1·75 mls* Direction of Racing:· *CLOCKWISE*
Max. Width *33ft* Solo   "
Min. Width *33ft* Sidecar   "
Number of Starters (Scratch):· Solo *40* S/Car *20*
Number of Starters (H/Cap):· Solo   S/Car

Method of Start *PUSH START*
DEAD ENGINE

CROPS
—x— SAFETY DITCH & BANK
▨ EARTH BANK
—·—· CHESTNUT FENCE

CAR PARK & SPECTATORS

CROSSING

TIMEKEEPERS OFFICE

PIT AREA

S/F

A

CAR PARK

CAR PARK

PADDOCK

SPECTATORS

SPECTATORS

BOUNDARY OF 4ft CHESTNUT FENCING

CAR PARK & SPECTATORS

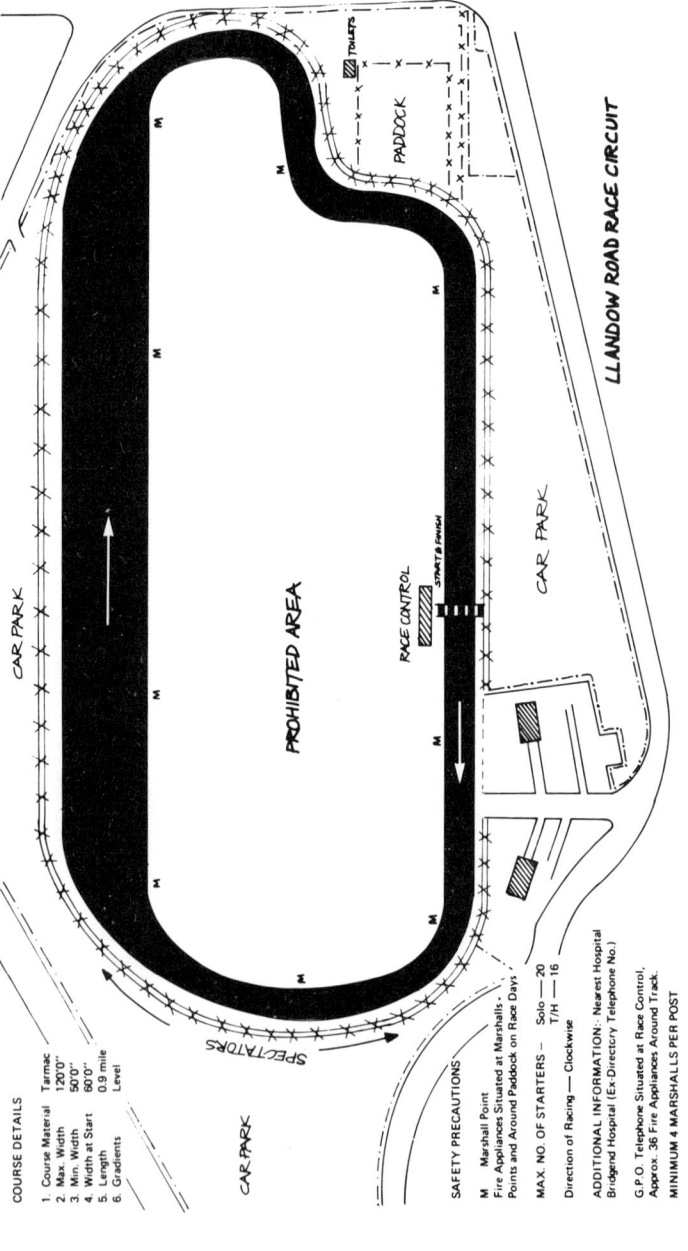

LLANDOW ROAD RACE CIRCUIT

COURSE DETAILS

1. Course Material — Tarmac
2. Max. Width — 120'0"
3. Min. Width — 50'0"
4. Width at Start — 60'0"
5. Length — 0.9 mile
6. Gradients — Level

SAFETY PRECAUTIONS

M Marshall Point
Fire Appliances Situated at Marshalls.
Points and Around Paddock on Race Days

MAX. NO. OF STARTERS — Solo — 20
                         T/H — 16

Direction of Racing — Clockwise

ADDITIONAL INFORMATION:- Nearest Hospital
Bridgend Hospital (Ex-Directory Telephone No.)

G.P.O. Telephone Situated at Race Control,
Approx. 36 Fire Appliances Around Track.

MINIMUM 4 MARSHALLS PER POST

PROHIBITED AREA

CAR PARK

SPECTATORS

RACE CONTROL

START & FINISH

PADDOCK

TOILETS

Chapter 11

Racing schools and practice

While production racing offers an obvious alternative to buying a pure racing machine with which to make your deput on the tarmac, there is one more alternative to diving straight in at the deep end of racing competition. There are in fact a couple of racing schools at which you can hire machines and the kit and receive instruction on every aspect of racing in the hands of experts, and where there are no embarrassing spectators or fellow competitors to unnerve you as they rush by.

They will guide the newcomer through all the first stages of racing at private training sessions on machines supplied by them and where you can also hire the riding equipment if necessary. When I say that it will cost you £10-£12 for the first time out that may sound awfully expensive but, again, just think what it could cost you if you went straight into the game. In fact it could cost you that for a days racing anyway once you are running your own machine, transporting it, putting the petrol into it and a van and paying the entry fees etc. etc, as detailed in the chapter on costs.

We'll tackle the Dixon school of racing first simply because they offer a variety of circuits whereas the Kirby-Camp school operates only at Brands Hatch.

The Dixon School holds sessions at Oulton Park, Silverstone, Lydden and Thruxton, apart from one held during TT weeks in the Isle of Man there were also sessions at tracks abroad to coincide with major Continental meetings. The operation is a three stage affair with the first comprising the theoretical instruction on the basic techniques followed by ten laps (eight at Thruxton) with the instructor and five on your own. The theory covers the lines through corners and the pitfalls to be avoided and how to get the best from the bike.

Questions will be answered, and while you are on the track everybody gets a chance to closely follow the instructor to see exactly where he peels off for a corner, where to brake etc. After you have completed laps by yourself you will get an unbiased assessment of your racing abilities - or lack of.

The essence of the assessment system is a set 'target' lap time for each circuit. It is a time set by the instructor for the circuit and conditions, which can be

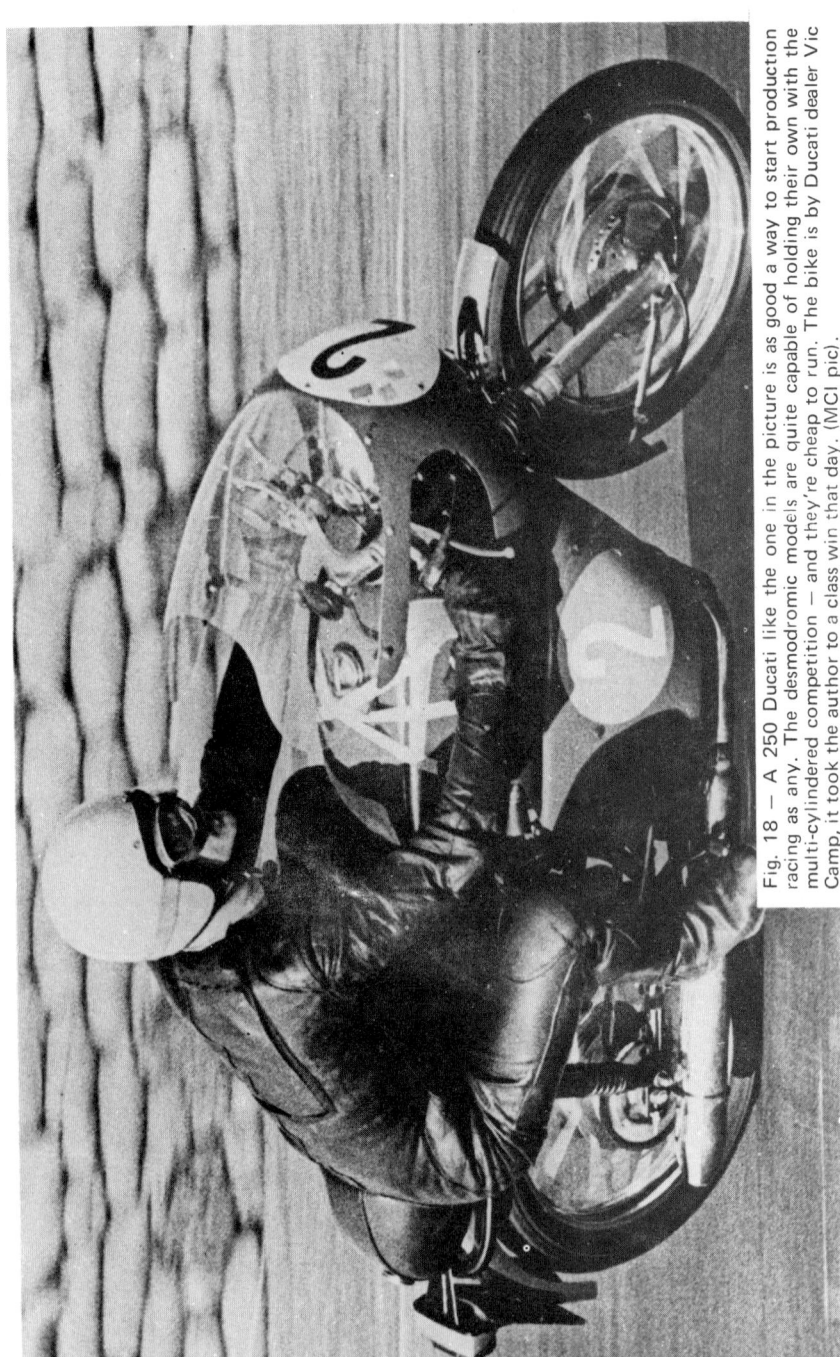

Fig. 18 — A 250 Ducati like the one in the picture is as good a way to start production racing as any. The desmodromic models are quite capable of holding their own with the multi-cylindered competition — and they're cheap to run. The bike is by Ducati dealer Vic Camp, it took the author to a class win that day. (MCI pic).

achieved by those with the ability, without having to ride on the limit. Those without some prospects of achieving competance will find it a hard target.

Having completed the first stage the next is speeded up to near racing conditions and to temper the overenthusiasm of some pupils a £5 deposit has to be lodged against your damaging the machine in the event that you 'chuck it up the road'. Stage three involves the use of a 450cc Honda in place of the 250s which are supplied to beginners. It's a 20 lap session in two parts. After the first the instructor will offer criticism and advice then he'll follow you round to see if you have learned the lessons.

There is quite a bit of 'fallout' to joining the school. There is a discount scheme where production of your membership card will get you reductions at certain dealers and persuading a friend to join the schools gets you extra free training laps on their machines. If you do happen to make the grade particularly well there is also the chance of being sponsored in a race by the school. The address to contact for more about this particular operation is as follows: Dixon Racing Ltd., 35 Wodeland Avenue, Guildford, Surrey. The prices as shown in their literature for the 1972 season were:

Stage one

Enrolment and the first 15 laps	-	£12.00
Additional five laps	-	£ 3.00
Additional ten laps	-	£ 5.00

Stage two (for those who have completed stage one and been recommended for stage two).   - £ 7.50

Additional five laps	-	£ 3.50
Additional ten laps	-	£ 5.50

Stage three (for those completing stage two satisfactorily).

First twenty laps	-	£15.00
Additional five laps	-	£ 4.00
Additional ten laps	-	£ 6.00

Fig. 19 — Big BMWs are rare in production racing. This one was privately entered in the TT and ridden by Helmut Dahne it finished fourth in the 750 class. Seen here at Quarter Bridge.

Hire of gear

Leathers	-	£ 1.25
Boots	-	£ .50
Helmet	-	£ .25

The Kirby-Camp International Racing School is the second such organisation and operates from Brands Hatch. Like the previous one it also supplies machines. In this case they are 250cc Ducati models, again in open racing tune, easy to ride and being four stroke machines needing no particular technique, so that the rider can concentrate on acquiring the necessary experience. It cost £10 in 1972 for the first 20 laps and if you are so unfortunate as to damage the machine then 50% of the repair bill may be yours. The prices for the hire of kit are similar except that leathers are £1.50. Addresses to contact for this one are: 10 Roneo Corner, Hornchurch, Essex. or 131 Queens Road, Walthamstow, London, E.17.

Open practice

There is one more possibility for trying the hard stuff without committing yourself to great expenditure or trouble, and that is to try riding round one of the circuits during an open practice session. These are held at many of the tracks and at Brands and Snetterton for instance you just turn up, sign-on, pay your money and away you go.

At the time of writing you could pay either £4 for a whole afternoon at Brands if you have some extensive testing to do, or really want to wear your bike out, or the arrangement might be that there are half hour sessions when solos go out, then 'chairs' or cars. Its best to phone the circuit to check which arrangements are in operation for the day you want. There might not be a session at all when you want to go, the tracks are hired by companies for private testing.

When you do go to these practice days supervision is minimal and its largely up to you so do remember to take those stands off and tape up lamp glasses. Watch out too for the inexperienced rider going too quickly for his own good, there are spills in practice too. The 'traffic', at Brands particularly, is sometimes heavy and the newcomer can find this distracting. It is of course a lot cheaper but you are on your own.

THE
PERFORMANCE
PAPERBACKS

are now published by

INTERAUTO

INTERAUTO BOOK COMPANY LTD

The following pages present to you some of the
current SpeedSport and Interauto books for the
motoring enthusiast, the automobile technician
and the motorist.

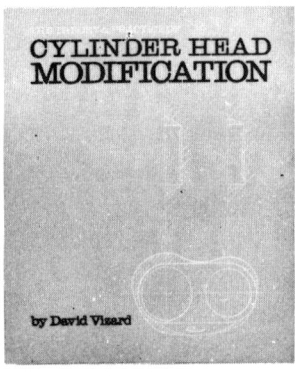

Motorsport

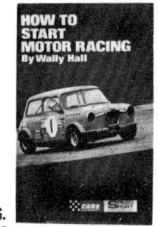

HOW TO START MOTOR RACING. Wally Hall. 011.9. £1.00

The author has had considerable club racing success and has passed on most of the vast experience he has gained. Ideal for anyone at all interested in beginning.

HOW TO START RALLYING. Colin Malkin. 024.0. £1.00

This famous rally driver takes the reader through all the mystiques of rally preparation. Car selection, suitability and setting up. Bodywork, lights, driving and navigation are some of the subjects dealt with. Colin co-drove the winning London to Sydney Marathon car.

HOW TO START AUTOCROSS AND RALLYCROSS. Peter Noad. 033.X. 80p

Like the rest of the 'How to Start' series but for the increasingly popular sport of autocross/rallycross. Like the other authors Peter Noad is an experienced and successful campaigner.

TOUCH WOOD. Duncan Hamilton. 042.9. £1.50

Paperback   25 b/w illustrations

We feel that we have found a great book in **TOUCH WOOD** and have re-issued it as the first title in our reprint series of motor racing classics. Duncan Hamilton was typical of the enthusiastic amateur who went racing for the sheer hell of it. He drove many makes of car to their limit, mostly Jaguars, utterly indifferent to his own safety and surviving many spectacular accidents. He won Le Mans at over 100 mph suffering from a monumental hangover, crashed an aeroplane, was torpedoed twice and helped to put England back on the motor racing map. His autobiography is a marvellous colourful story and has been out of print for a long time.

HOW TO START PRODUCTION MOTOR CYCLE RACING Ray Knight 030.5 £1.00
Ray Knight

Ray Knight is a journalist with 10 years racing, a TT win and lap record to his credit. He passes all his experience to the enthusiast. 'A good guide to success.'

THE *BARRY LEE* BOOK OF HOT ROD RACING   062.3   £1.00

Barry Lee revolutionised Hot Rod Racing in 1970 and in 1971 became British Champion, as well as making successful forays to Denmark and South Africa. In his book Barry Lee shows how he built his Escort, what it's like in a hot rod race, where and when hot rod racing takes place - in fact he writes about everything that an intending competitor, a hot rod fan or spectator will want to know.

Marque tuning guides

TUNING THE MINI.   Clive Trickey   **001.0. £1.00**
The Mini Tuners' Bible; universally recognised as the most authoritative
book on the subject. The most popular marque tuning book to be
published.

MORE MINI TUNING.   Clive Trickey   **000.3. £1.00**
New! The second edition of the companion volume to 'Tuning the Mini'.
Updated with much more information on valve gear, carbs, camshafts
and gearboxes.

TUNING STANDARD TRIUMPHS up to 1300 cc.   **012.7. 50p**
Richard Hudson-Evans
Essential reading for Herald, Spitfire, 1300, Standard 8 and 10 owners.
Full tuning information.

TUNING STANDARD TRIUMPHS over 1300 cc.   **029.1. £1.60p**
David Vizard
The tuning stages for Vitesses, GT6, TRs and all 2000 units from stage 1
to full race.

TUNING VOLKSWAGENS.   Peter Noad   **026.7. £1.00**
An expert guide to the race and rally preparations of VWs; it covers the
various types of car and their development and competition history.
Includes a section on Beach Buggies.

TUNING ESCORTS AND CAPRIS.   David Vizard   **009.7. £1.00**
The technical editor of 'Cars and Car Conversions' explains engine and
chassis tuning procedures for both road and track.

TUNING ANGLIAS AND CORTINAS.   **003.8. 80p**
This bestseller deals with engine and chassis tuning and details the early
Classic and Capri, the V4 and Twin Cam power units.

TUNING TWIN CAM FORDS.   David Vizard   **007.0. 80p**
The stage-by-stage modifications for these engines, from 'warm' 1600s
to full-race 1800s. Fully illustrated.

TUNING BMC SPORTS CARS.   Mike Garton   **004.6. 80p**
The author, once a technical expert at British Leyland Special Tuning
Department passes his wealth of experience on to the interested owner.

TUNING IMPS.   Willy Griffiths   **052.6. 50p**
The Imp is one of the most difficult cars to modify. The author lets out
all the secrets on what can and cannot be done. **NEW 2nd Edition.**

TUNING VIVAS AND FIRENZAS Blydenstein & Coburn **064.X** **£1.00**
Written by the country's leading experts, this is the first tuning book on
these popular cars. It covers all aspects of tuning for both road and
track.

TUNING V8 ENGINES.   David Vizard   **028.3. £1.50p**
This book covers the principles involved for modifying a large selection
of V8 engines— design trends, supercharging, assembly, part swapping,
carburation etc.

TUNING SIDE VALVE FORDS.   Bill Cooper   **005.4. 80p**
This book covers the 100E engine fitted to early Ford Anglias and
Prefects now finding their way into many youthful hands.

BUILDING AND RACING AN 850 MINI.   Clive Trickey. **010.1. £1.00**
Another winner from Clive Trickey who describes here the story of his own
racing success in a step-by-step method that can be followed by the would-be
racer.

Carburetter guide

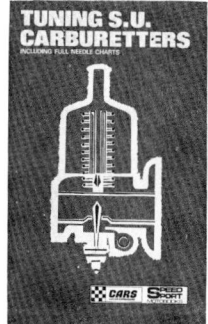

TUNING SU CARBURETTERS. 017.8.   70p
The SU carburetter is fitted to all BLMC cars and is often used for carburetter conversions to tuned cars. This book is a complete guide to their tuning, servicing and fitting, with recommended jets and full needle charts, both for the enthusiast and economy-minded motorist. Recommended by the Manufacturer.

WEBER CARBURETTERS.   John Passini.   018.6.   70p
This book covers the setting-up, method of operation and servicing on one of the finest carburetters available for high performance engines. Written by an acknowledged specialist on these carbs.

TUNING STROMBERG CARBURETTERS.   006.2.   70p
A similar volume to the SU carburetter book but for tuning the very popular Stromberg carburetter. Again recommended by the Manufacturer.

WEBER CARBURETTERS
Part 2 - Tuning and Maintenance   John Passini   060.7   70p

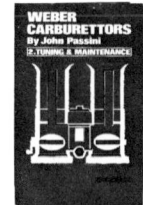

This is the companion volume to the very successful Weber Carbs book by the same author, which dealt with the Theory of how Webers worked and functioned only. John Passini has worked very closely with the factory to provide in this book all there is to know about Weber tuning and maintenance. Profusely illustrated and complete with needle, settings and application data tables.

and soon to follow: TUNING SOLEX CARBURETTERS

TUNING COMPANION SERIES

TUNING LUCAS IGNITION SYSTEMS   063.1   £ 1.00

This book examines each component in the Lucas ignition system and explains how to test and check that it is functioning correctly. Also dealt with are the special procedures and requirements of systems on high performance engines, with setting up instructions, trouble shooting hints and comprehensive data tables.

INTRODUCTION TO TUNING. 002.X. 50p
ENGINES AND TRANSMISSIONS. 013.5. 50p
SUSPENSIONS AND BRAKES. 027.5. 50p

Martyn Watkins has written a basic guide to the tuning and modification of production cars. These three volumes of the **TUNING COMPANION** series are designed to take the beginner through the theory and then the practice stage by stage. They should then lead him into the more detailed work featured in the rest of the Motobook range.

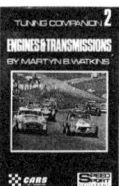 

AUTO ELECTRICS. David Westgate. 014.3. £ 1.00
A well illustrated and easily readable guide to the car's electrical system. This book should be a standard work as it covers all aspects of this complicated subject from batteries to ammeters.

CAR CUSTOMISING. Paul Cockburn. 031.3. 90p
A new book on this increasingly popular form of car modification. Paul Cockburn a brilliant young designer explains the ground work and suggests many practical ideas.

MODIFYING PRODUCTION CYLINDER HEADS.
Clive Trickey. 008.9. 50p
Clive Trickey's famous basic guide to the modification of cylinder heads for improved performance. A standard work which has become a best seller.

RACING ENGINE PREPARATION. Clive Trickey. 015.1. £ 1.00
Fully describes the conversion of mass-produced engines to full blown racing units.

New edition
Castrol Book
of Car Care

SBN 902-587-005
This is the new edition of the ever popular Castrol Book of Car Care in a new format and at a new price.
'Car Care' has been rewritten and considerably updated, with new drawings, diagrams and photographs. It now has a full-colour cover.
'Car Care' does exactly what its title suggests under the following chapter headings:
1. A Happy Partnership? 2. Servicing; 3. Bodywork; 4. Engine; 5. Transmission; 6. Brakes; 7. Suspension and Steering; 8. Tyres; 9. Electrics; 10. Breakdown Trouble-shooter; 11. Safety and Security; 12. Castrol at your Service.

25p

The Big Drive

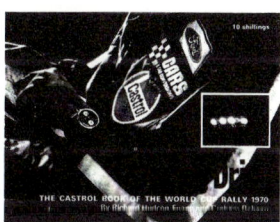

THE BIG DRIVE.
Richard Hudson-Evans and Graham Robson.
032.1. 50p
The Book of the World Cup Rally, 1970.
The first behind-the-wheel view of the toughest rally ever—the car breaking London to Mexico Race.

Castrol book

'TWO WHEELER CARE'
a sister publication to the 'Castrol Book of Car Care' describes the various parts of the machine tells what they are designed to do and suggests the best course of action for looking after them. Used intelligently it can save a lot of time, money and frustration.
Still very popular and a constant best seller.

25p

HOW TO KEEP YOUR VW ALIVE. John Muir. £2.50
'A manual of step by step procedures for the complete idiot'
Softback, ring-bound, profusely illustrated

This brilliant book has been a huge success in America. It is written by an expert engineer who appreciates that complex technical procedures cannot be followed by the amateur mechanic. He explains how to look after a VW in simple language combined with a wry humour.
Basically a manual, but very different from any others. Extremely valuable even though unusual in approach. It is proving that the success in America was no flash in the pan.

General Motoring

"I imagine the signs will bring quicker reaction from fellow motorists on a motorway than any amount of gesticulating or pitiful messages written on the back of an envelope."
Bradford Telegraph.

".....this could prove to be a big selling line."
Auto Accessory International.

EMERGENCY SIGNS FOR MOTORISTS
ISBN: 0-903192-08-X Size: 11¾ '' x 8¼''

A book of easily-recognizable poster-size emergency signs which can save the user time and embarrassment by showing passing motorists that something is wrong. There is a sign appertaining to almost all situations — everything, in fact, from an 'ON TOW' notice to a hazard warning sign. Perhaps of most importance is the inclusion of signs relating directly to accident prevention and the need for medical assistance. A sign such as 'DOCTOR WANTED', displayed with a large cross, attracts immediate attention and is easily understood.

Officially approved by the Design Centre and featured on the television show **"Drive In"**, EMERGENCY SIGNS FOR MOTORISTS provides a service which is long overdue and which, as our roads grow ever more crowded, should become an essential item in the responsible driver's equipment. Remember: It will be worth more than its price when you need it!

"Useful when you break down"
Sunday Telegraph.

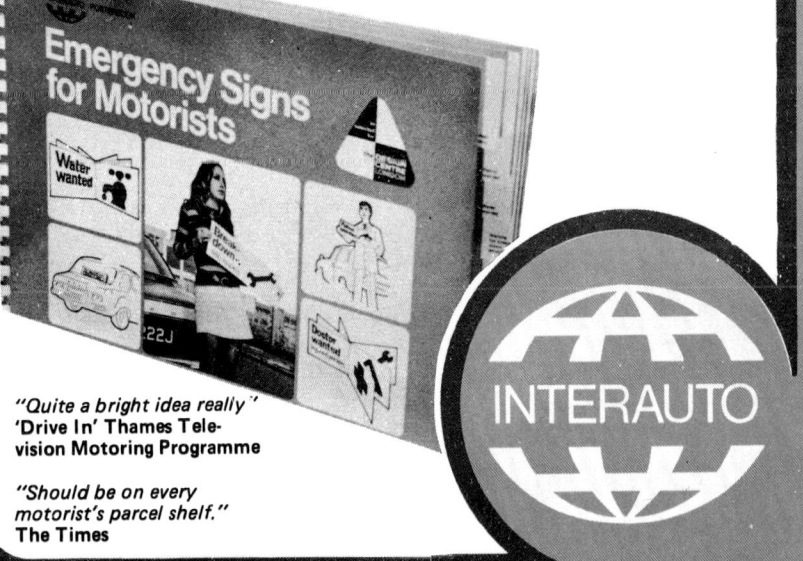

"Quite a bright idea really"
'Drive In' Thames Television Motoring Programme

"Should be on every motorist's parcel shelf."
The Times

INTERAUTO

Workshop Series

A range of books on important but much-neglected aspects of automotive technology for the engineer and mechanic.

PETROL FUEL INJECTION SYSTEMS
ISBN: 0-903192-20-9
Size: 8½" x 11"
380 pages Illustrated
One of the first books published containing detailed information on the construction and operation of most of the major petrol fuel injection systems available today. The opening section deals with the development of the first P.I. Systems, dating as far back as 1940. This is followed by descriptive information and technical data on various systems available on the

present day market. Finally, service information on a number of vehicles to

which a P.I. System has been fitted.
With an abundance of clearly laid-out photographs, drawings and plans, and in the same large format as the other titles in the series, this book covers: AE BRICO, BOSCH (Mechanical and Electronic), KUGEL-FISHER, LUCAS & TECALEMIT in relation to the motor vehicles equipped with these systems.

ALTERNATOR SERVICE MANUAL
ISBN: 0-903192-28-4
Size: 8½" x 11"
250 pages Illustrated
This valuable publication for automotive electricians deals extensively with the testing and maintenance of Alternators and Regulators. Compiled from genuine manufacturers' service manuals.
CONTENTS: Alternator technology Bosch, Butec, CAV, Chrysler, Delco, Remy, Email, Fiat, Ford, Hitachi, Leece-Neville, Lucas, Mitsubishi.
Motorola & Prestolite Application tables listing current vehicles and their standard alternators, for easy cross reference.

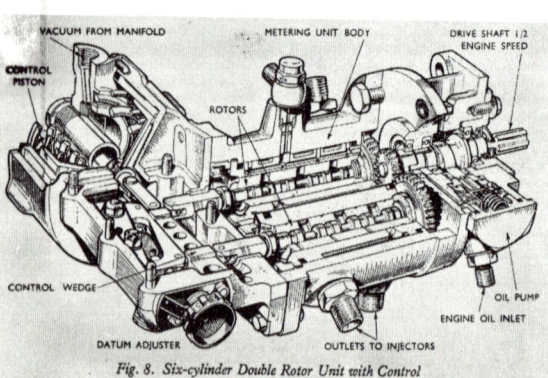

Fig. 8. Six-cylinder Double Rotor Unit with Control

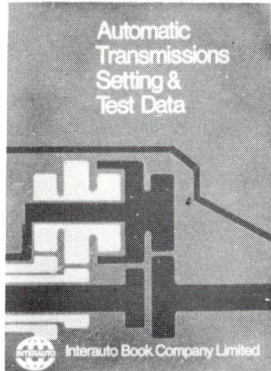

Automatic
Transmissions
Setting &
Test Data

Interauto Book Company Limited

Crypton
Triangle
(Transervice)
Publications

**AUTOMATIC TRANS-
MISSION SETTING AND
TEST DATA**
ISBN: 0-903192-29-2
Size: 8½" x 11"
150 pages

Presented in a compact and
easy-to-read format are
the setting and testing
procedures for the more
popular automatic trans-
mission systems in their
adapted form for use in
the majority of vehicles.
Additionally, the book
contains such information
as pressure tables, shift
speeds, the location of
pressure take-off points,
plus comprehensive fault
diagnosis charts which
enable the user to carry
out checks and adjustments
with speed and accuracy.

The subject of automatic
transmission is a complex
one. This publication does
not purport to be a work-
shop manual dealing with
system overhaul and
repair, but it will prove of
great value to the service
engineer involved in the
final on-car setting and
testing.

Transmission lists by
vehicle make and model as
cross-reference.

'Engine and Electrical Service'
over 250 pages and 450 illu-
strations   £ 2.50

'Corrective Service'
a new approach to fault finding
that interprets all oscilloscope
traces and meter indications   £ 2.50

'Diagnostic Wallchart'
40"x30", for quick reference, it
shows all oscilloscope traces
and related fault conditions   £ 2.50

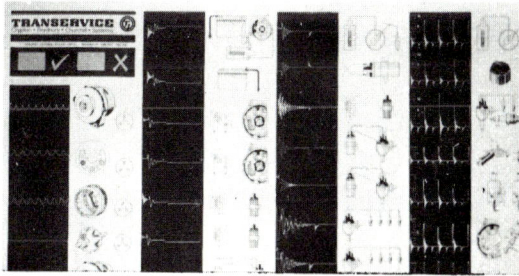

WALL CHART
40" x 30" three colour chart showing all oscilloscope traces.
Ideal for checking "fault" conditions.

Interauto Books
for the professional

All priced at 95p

Interauto Automobile Engineering Reference Series

These books are directed at the car mechanic, the apprentice, the technician and the more experienced do-it-yourself motorist. In clear language, and with numerous illustrations, each title fully details a specific motor engineering subject. All books written by leading motor engineering experts and revised in accordance with 1971/2 technologies.

Part of the series was originally published in Germany by Vogel Verlag, one of that country's largest technical publishers, who have already sold more than 100,000 copies. Licensed editions of the series are also published in Spanish and Dutch.

Each book is designed to be carried around for constant and immediate reference and its handy format facilitates this. Research with major technical booksellers has shown that no reference series of this type has previously been available and that there consequently exists an unlimited demand and sales potential. A further advantage is that the series covers a truly international selection of vehicle systems.

Current titles in this series:

Automobile Fault Diagnosis
Automobile Radio Interference Suppression
Automobile Body & Paintwork Repairs
Automobile Engine Testing
Automobile Performance Testing
Automobile Diagnostic Testing

Automobile Braking Systems
Bosch Electrical Systems
Caravans - Function, Servicing, Repairs

S.U. Carburetters — Testing, Servicing, Overhauls
Zenith Carburetters — Testing, Servicing, Overhauls
Stromberg Carburetters — Testing, Servicing, Overhauls
Solex Carburetters — Testing, Servicing, Overhauls

(other carburetter books are in preparation)

HOW TO ORDER
Motobooks

Whenever you wish to purchase any of the listed books take this form to your Bookseller or Motorshop who will order the book for you. If this is not possible, mail the order form to us with your payment and we will send the required books to you by return.

Please observe the following instructions:

		ALBION SCOTT LTD.·
		Bercourt House
ORDERING		51 York Road
BOOKS	from	Brentford Middx
BY MAIL		TW8 OQP England

Identify required books on this form.
Mail complete form to us, with your remittance (either cheque, postal order or cash) to which you must add the postage as set out below.

Make sure that your
  NAME and ADDRESS is given in the space below.

Postage and Packing:

		UK	EUROPE	OVERSEAS
Book price to	£2.00	10p	15p	20p
	£3.00	15p	20p	25p
over	£3.00	20p	30p	40p

Dispatch by surface book mail only.

Name ....

Address ....

Special Instructions ....

Get your facts straight from a Motobook

ORDER FORM

SPECIAL TITLES FROM ALBION SCOTT

Qty	Title	Price	Total	Qty	Title	Price	Total
	SPEEDSPORT				**INTERAUTO**		
	Tuning SU Carburetters	70p			Fault Diagnosis	95p	
	Tuning Weber, Part 1	70p			Interference Suppression	95p	
	Tuning Weber, Part 2	70p			Body and Paintwork	95p	
	Tuning Stromberg	70p			Performance Testing	95p	
	Tuning the Mini	£1.00			Engine Testing	95p	
	More Mini Tuning	£1.00			Braking Systems	95p	
	850 Mini	£1.00			Bosch Electrical Systems	95p	
	Four Cylinder Fords	£1.00			Diagnostic Testing	95p	
	Anglias and Cortinas	80p					
	Tuning Twin Cam Fords	80p					
	Tuning Side Valve Fords	80p			SU Carburetters	95p	
	Escorts and Capris	£1.00			Solex Carburetters	95p	
	Tuning Vivas & Firenzas	£1.00			Zenith Carburetters	95p	
	Tuning BMC Sports Cars	80p			Stromberg Carburetters	95p	
	Triumphs to 1300cc	50p			Weber Carburetters	95p	
	Tuning the VW	£1.00					
	Tuning Imps	50p					
	Tuning V8 Engines	£1.50			Caravans	95p	
	How to Start Rallying	£1.00			Alternator Manual	£2.50	
	Barry Lee Hot Rod	£1.00			Automatic Transm Data	£2.50	
	HS Motor Racing	80p			Petrol Fuel Injection	£3.80	
	How to Start Autocross	80p					
	Prod. Motorcy Racing	£1.00			Better Motoring Yearbk	95p	
	Introduction to Tuning	50p			Motorist Emerg Signs	75p	
	Engines and Transm	50p					
	Suspensions and Brakes	50p			**CRYPTON**		
	Auto Electrics	£1.00			Engine and Electrical	£2.50	
	Lucas Ignition Systems	£1.00			Transistors in Motor	95p	
	Modif. Prod. Cy Heads	50p			Corrective Service	£2.50	
	Racing Engine Prep	£1.00			Oscilloscopes in Engine	95p	
	Car Customising	£1.00			Diagnostic Wallchart	£2.50	
	High Speed Driving	£1.50			WORKSHOP MANUAL		
	Cylinder Head Modific	£2.40			quote make, model & year	£2.00	
	Scramble	£1.00			HANDBOOK		
	Open Cockpit	£1.00			quote make, model & year	75p	
	Hot Air Ballooning	£1.50					
	Touch Wood	£1.40			Better Motoring Yearbk	95p	
	Keep Your VW Alive	£2.50			Motorist Emerg Signs	75p	
	The Big Drive	50p					
	Castrol Bk of Car Care	25p					
	Motorcycle Care	25p					
	Qty TOTAL Price				**Qty TOTAL Price**		

NOTES. _____

_____